What People Are Saying  ;, ACC

"Darcy has coached and mentored associ   :vels and in each case has demonstrated a unique a_____those associates to new levels of performance and engagement. She quickly helps you see situations from different perspectives, identify potential alternatives, solutions or ideas, and asks questions that get you moving down a positive path. Darcy is a consummate professional and I would strongly recommend her to anyone seeking an effective coach or mentor."

Ray Baumruk, AonHewitt
Lincolnshire, Illinois

"Darcy is an outstanding leadership coach. She listens intently, assesses quickly and accurately, and has the remarkable ability to instantly crystallize vague ideas into solid and actionable concepts. Her energy and enthusiasm are inspiring, her kindness and sincerity are heartwarming, and her intellect is broad and deep. In short, you can trust Darcy to help you find your way forward."

April Bogle, Emory University
Atlanta, Georgia

"I'm struck by Darcy's unparalleled gift of zooming in on what's most germane to guide you through exploring the best way to reach your personal and professional goals. When you work with Darcy you'll examine, discover, dream, prioritize and do your homework. In the end, her fresh thinking makes your career path feel like a walk in the park on a sunny day—a pleasant experience you look forward to!"

Monica M. Zimmer, APR, Sodexo
Bethesda, Maryland

"Working with Coach Darcy has helped us bring more clarity and effective action to our business, and is pushing our firm to new heights that we couldn't have reached without her."

John K. Ritter, CFP, CFS, Ritter Daniher Financial Advisory
Cincinnati, Ohio

"Darcy has a true gift for listening and bringing out the best in her clients. Her coaching style is nurturing, yet she challenges you to reach outside your comfort zone and awaken strengths in you that you may not realize you have. The results can be personally enlightening, and help you to explore career opportunities that may have seemed beyond your reach."

Allyse Denmark, AMEC
Atlanta, Georgia

"Darcy has been blessed with the ability to effectively communicate from both sides of a conversation. Whether coaching or inspiring others via her blog, speaking engagements, or one-on-one mentoring, she never ceases to provide great information that applies to the universe of situations we all face in our lives."

Andrew Pollock, GISP, Booz Allen Hamilton
Marietta, Georgia

"Darcy is a great coach! Working with her was just what I needed to get me unstuck and moving forward in my business. Darcy helped to bring clarity around what I needed to focus on and she held me accountable as I achieved my goals. She asked thought-provoking questions and offered practical solutions. I left each session feeling energized and ready to take action."

Michelle O'Donnell, SPHR, ACC
Atlanta, Georgia

"Darcy has a knack for getting to the nub of the matter—reading her writing is like unlocking a chest full of truths that other writers would take much longer to open."

Tom Auclair, professional stage and screen actor
Denver, Colorado

"Darcy is amazing! I've experienced firsthand, and seen in others, the dramatic effect of her powerful insights and advice. I've adapted as my own so many of the things I've learned from her that I frequently find myself repeating them when advising and coaching others. Her influence—her raw power—to encourage and inspire people to achieve, improve and succeed extends well beyond those she has coached or mentored directly."

Cheli Brown, Aon Hewitt
Atlanta, Georgia

"Darcy's insight and observations into human behavior really shine when she describes how people can overcome the obstacles to their success, whether those obstacles are internal or external."

Dan Martin, Licensed Professional Counselor
Sydney, Australia

"Darcy is an exceptional mentor and coach! I grew tremendously as a manager under her excellent coaching. She was always able to offer exceptional insight into issues and opportunities. Darcy challenged me to always think of different perspectives, and to adapt my skills to the needs of my clients and my colleagues."

Doug Browning, Kaiser Permanente
Honolulu, Hawaii

BRING YOUR SUPERPOWERS TO WORK^{SM}

Your Guide
to More Clarity,
Confidence &
Control

DARCY EIKENBERG, ACC
Founder, RedCapeRevolution.com

Published by Red Cape Revolution Media, a division of RedCapeRevolution.com.

Book cover and text design created in conjunction with DoneForYouPublishing.com.

This is the first edition. If you'd like to make a suggestion for future editions, please visit our website at www.RedCapeRevolution.com, or contact us:
- Facebook (www.Facebook.com/RedCapeRevolution),
- LinkedIn (www.LinkedIn.com/in/DarcyEikenberg) or
- Twitter (@RedCapeRev).

For inquiries about speaking engagements, media appearances or bulk purchases of this book, email info@RedCapeRevolution.com or call (404) 857-2REV (2738).

Library of Congress Control Number 2011919505
ISBN# 978-0-9839874-0-6

About the Author

Innovative yet practical, creative yet structured, fun yet results-focused, Darcy Eikenberg can really only be described in one way: She shows people how to get more life out of work.

With a unique mix of perspectives, passions, and practice as a leadership and workplace coach, author, mentor, and speaker, Darcy founded the Red Cape Revolution (*www.RedCapeRevolution.com*) as a way to help everyday professionals rediscover their own superpowers, bring them to their work, and make a bigger difference in their corner of the world.

She is recognized for her ability to motivate and inspire today's busy professionals to create new ways to gain more clarity, build more confidence, and take more control at work, in ways that work for their organizations and for themselves.

To learn more, see Darcy's Story in the Extras section of this book, or visit *www.RedCapeRevolution.com.*

Are You Ready to Bring Your Superpowers to Work?

Get Your Special Bonus Resources Now!

www.RedCapeRevolution.com/BookBonus

While this book is filled with ideas you can put into practice right away, we want you to have even more tools to help you bring your superpowers to work and start soaring through your career and life! So, whether you're overdue for a change in your worklife or are just starting to think about it, go grab your free resources at *www.RedCapeRevolution.com/BookBonus*.

Here's what you'll find:

- Darcy's companion video, *Getting Started with the Red Cape Revolution*, will walk you through this book and help you grab the highlights. It's a brief overview and also a good reminder later when you need a refresher.

- Our Frequently Asked Questions (FAQs), updated regularly with answers to questions from readers just like you.

- A special link where you can send your questions about the ideas in the book directly to Darcy and her Red Cape Revolution team. It's an opportunity to get personal answers and attention that may change your own experiences at work.

- Invitations to ongoing events, workshops, and classes where you can continue to build your clarity, confidence, and control at work.

Plus, the Red Cape Revolution team adds special surprises and bonuses all the time, exclusive to readers and fans of this book, so check it out today!

To Mom, Dad, and Dana, who help me keep
my red cape flying strong
even when the winds are stilled.
I love you all.

Contents

Introduction

Remember when you were a kid, and you played superhero? You put your red cape around your shoulders, and—wham-o! —you could use your powers to change the world. Or maybe just the backyard.

And then you grew up, and tossed the cape in the back of the closet. You zipped up your school clothes, buttoned up your work clothes, and started walking the path everyone thought you should. And in most cases, that path was, well, just fine. Not superb. Not awful. Just fine.

Suddenly, the world started shifting under your feet. Maybe you got laid off. Maybe you got divorced or stayed single longer, or someone close to you got sick, or died. Maybe you celebrated a birthday that had a big fat zero on the end. Maybe your company evaporated overnight in scandal or was replaced by new innovations. Maybe your job stayed secure, but you found yourself spending more time managing the rumor mill than managing your business.

Nothing seemed clear anymore—not even the things you always assumed would be the same. Your confidence became shaky, at best. And control? Increasingly, an illusion.

So you started asking yourself some questions—big questions, hard questions, like "How did I get here?" and "Is this all there is?" At first, the questions sound like static on the radio, but eventually, they tune in, softly—so soft that the buzz of your BlackBerry can still drown them out. Weeks pass, and they've grown a little louder, a little bolder, a little more urgent. Finally, the questions start shouting inside your brain. They're demanding an answer from you—right now. What should you do?

The answer is to put your red cape back on. The answer is to regain the **clarity**, rebuild the **confidence**, and take back the **control** you need to *be*—and *feel*—successful in the new world of work.

The answer is to join the Red Cape Revolution, and start bringing your superpowers to work.

PART
1

Welcome to the Red Cape Revolution

Have you ever known someone—maybe a colleague, a friend, or even yourself—who felt stuck in his work, trapped, maybe even frustrated—even though to the outside world it looked like he was very successful, like everything was going great?

Have you ever heard someone wish she could just wave a magic wand, take a giant leap, make a bold change—but then tell herself she can't possibly do it because it'd be too risky, too expensive, or too overwhelming?

And, have you ever stood by and watched this person stay stuck, day after day, month after month, year after year?

I know that person. In fact, I *was* that person. And I found out the hard way that it sucks for air to be that person.

Sorry to be so blunt, but if you're this person right now, I want you to know that you don't have to stay that way. I didn't.

In fact, now, after lots of dedicated work, wise advice, and big leaps of faith, I have the good fortune to coach and teach people—people like you, your colleagues, and friends—the practical, simple, yet powerful ways I discovered to revolutionize your work and career without screwing up everything in your life.

It's my privilege to welcome you to the Red Cape Revolution, where we bring our superpowers to work for ourselves, our companies, our communities, and our world.

Why We're Here

After going through the shock of radical, fast change in recent years, the world of work has been shifting—not just rumbling, but dramatically changing shape and form right under our feet.

Just like with any other seismic activity, a tremor here causes craters over there. And so the rumbles of change have dug craters in our attitudes about work. Those craters have echoed in now-everyday conversations like these:

- "Keep your head down and don't make waves," advises your colleague.

- "Go along to get along," says your spouse.

- "Be thankful you have a job," says your mother.

All these tidbits of well-meaning advice have one thing in common: They're based on **fear**. Fear of losing a job, an income, a reputation, control. Fear of the unknown, of the next tremor. Fear that maybe next time the earth shakes, we won't be left standing.

Fear is likely one reason why you're holding this book in your hands right now. You long for an antidote to fear, a way back to a normal that you know doesn't exist.

We can't give in to the fear. When we do, we're playing possum, staying still, taking the passive route. And passive behavior creates nothing.

- No innovation.

- No creativity.

- No new income.

- No operational breakthroughs.

- No satisfaction.

- No enjoyment.

- No fulfillment.

- No love.

Do you *really* want to work like that? Maybe you're not sure there's any other way.

My goal here is to show you that there is. I want to prove to you that you can stand in the three-way intersection of a successful career, a successful life, and a successful organization without getting run over in the process. Now *that's* revolutionary.

I also want to show you why it's so important, and why you can't wait one more day to get started. I want you to know why it matters.

Why it Matters

You're a smart person, and you probably recognize that it's not quite right for you to fritter away your time, energy, money, and talent too much. But maybe you aren't sure exactly why. Maybe you think it has something to do with "profit" or "productivity." Nope. It actually has to do with another p-word: problems.

Yes, there are a lot of problems in our world. (Maybe in your company they call them "challenges" or "opportunities.") Let's just face it—a bunch of things are broken.

Each of us is witness to these problems all the time, big and small. Across the desk, across the street, or across the ocean, these problems can feel huge, overwhelming, and out of our reach. They make us worry, lose sleep, and, in some situations, even make us physically sick.

Yes, I see the problems. But at the same time, I see the solution.

In my work as a leadership and workplace coach and speaker, I have the great joy to be invited into rooms—conference rooms, offices, auditoriums, church basements, banquet halls, break rooms, theaters, you name it. And there are *people* in these rooms. (If you picked up this book, maybe you've been one of them.) It's my honor to be there and talk to these people, teach a little, and listen a lot.

In these rooms, I learn about the great things people are doing every single day in their worklives, even if they're not convinced those things are so great. I see sparks of new ideas flickering. I watch the energy coursing through their veins when a possibility gets them excited. I feel the passion and motivation loaded within their hands, heads, and hearts. They're ready to burst.

But they don't. And our problems go on.

Holding Us Back: The Three Little Lies

So why doesn't every drop of that talent, skill, ability, passion, innovation, creativity, smarts, energy, etc.—things I call your superpowers, which you'll read more about in Part 2—constantly explode across all of our problems, shredding our troubles to pieces (or at least to more manageable sizes)? Why does so much of that good, valuable, in-demand stuff seem to stay locked up?

I wasn't sure. I knew what had happened to me—how I got stuck, and what it took to get me moving in the right direction—but I thought, "Well, perhaps that's just me." I saw what happened to my clients, and wondered, "Well, perhaps that's just them." Then I started doing additional research and asking deeper questions of people who had broken through—people who were solving problems in new and different ways. Mostly, though, I kept doing my coaching, speaking, and teaching work, showing up in those rooms, and paying close attention.

Over time, I heard what was holding people back. I discovered that these amazing people tell themselves three little lies that keep them standing still, keeping their gifts and assets tight in their grasp rather than flinging them more broadly into the world. The three little lies are:

- "It will be too hard."
- "I'm too busy."
- "I'm too lazy to make the effort."

Sound familiar? Do you tell yourself it'll be too hard—even though you know you're perfectly capable of hard work? Are you in the "too busy" camp, yet let pockets of time escape to complaining, Internet surfing, or reality TV? And don't tell me you're lazy; I see what you do each and every day to keep up with your current life.

Now, I don't think you mean to lie to yourself. Maybe you've just listened to others who have accepted these lies as fact for too long. Or maybe you believe these lies because you've seen no proof to the contrary. (Whew—it's a good thing you're reading this book, then. You'll get your proof and hopefully become someone else's proof, someday soon.)

So let's look at what it'll take to break through these lies, and start bringing your superpowers to work.

Moving Us Forward: The Three Keys

Lies exposed, I started looking for ways to unlock the superpowers I've witnessed in those many rooms. I wanted to know the secrets that everyday professionals like you and me could use without changing every single thing in our lives.

I found these three keys:

- Clarity.

- Confidence.

- Control.

They seem so simple on the surface, right? Well, if clarity, confidence, and control were simple to have and use, I think more of us would be using them already. But instead, I found many of us fall into one or more of the following categories:

- We lack clarity about our superpowers, and what we want to do with them, doubting what makes us unique, special, and amazing;

- We lack confidence, waiting for external permission and validation from someone, somewhere, instead of granting it to ourselves; and

- We assume we have no control, when in reality, we control everything we do, say, and think—and that's a lot.

Let's take a closer look at these three keys of clarity, confidence, and control, because they are at the heart of wearing your red cape and bringing your superpowers to work.

Why Clarity?

Knowing and really owning your superpowers is .. your name. You identify with it, are proud of it, and don't hes... to use it. When you get crystal clear about the unique and special forces within you, you can make better choices about where you invest your most valuable resources: your time, energy, money, emotion, and attention.

When you have clarity, it's so much simpler to say "yes" to some investments and "no" to others—even at work. Plus, there's an extra added bonus: "No" becomes a more acceptable answer, and saying no can be guilt-free.

When you get clear about your superpowers, you also clear away the things that don't matter—things you know are not your problems to solve, your mountains to climb, your projects to lead, your challenges to tackle. You get to say "no" to many things with ease because you are ultra-clear about who you are, and what's most important for you to do and contribute.

When you claim your superpowers, you suddenly explode with a realm of possibilities that weren't there before. The old line "nature abhors a vacuum" is true here. When you get clear about and eliminate what doesn't matter, you create space for new opportunities and ideas to erupt.

Why Confidence?

Ah, the elusive seed! Why is it that everyone admires confidence and wants more of it, but no one ever seems to get enough of it?

By definition, confidence is "trust, a state of being certain." Well, it's no wonder we're in a confidence deficit today—we live in a state when nothing seems certain. In a generation where "bank" has become a four-letter word, we can all use a good hit of confidence.

Knowing your superpowers brings you confidence. Understanding the difference you make, or the effect you have, or the change you create—all of those results generate an internal knowing, the confidence you long for. You know how to talk about what's unique and special about you, how use those superpowers, and how to see the difference you can make at your workplace, in your community, and even in the world.

The beautiful part is that others long to be confident in us, too, and are naturally attracted to the secure, heads-up individual. They see your high confidence quotient and it makes them more confident in you, which in turn increases your own confidence even more. What a deal! When you use your superpowers as a baseline for all you do, your confidence shines through.

Why Control?

Many things that keep us up at night—illness, financial devastation, natural disasters, terrorism—speak to our inherent need to want some level of control over our lives. We're not really afraid of the potential accident; we're afraid the accident will take away our control over our body, mind, or other abilities. **We fear what we can't control.**

In fact, in Daniel Pink's powerful book *Drive: The Surprising Truth About What Motivates Us,* he cites significant behavioral research proving that the need for autonomy—or, the ability to have choice and control over our own lives—is one of the main elements that motivates human behavior.

The truth is that ***all*** you can control is what you choose to do, say, and think. Say that with me: "All I can control is what I choose to do, say, and think." That's it. So discovering your superpowers, and getting that clarity and confidence in place, targets the things you're doing, saying, and thinking even further.

And in the workplace, when we're doing, saying, and thinking the things that are in line with our unique superpowers, that are red cape–ready, we have the best chance we can get of creating and holding onto control of any situation we encounter.

- We make the right choices for us—not choices based on what others say.

- We do work we care about—and stop doing what we don't.

- We know when we've gotten ourselves out of control— and know how to get back on track.

Do you have these three keys of clarity, confidence, and control already rattling around in your briefcase? If not, would you like to? I'm betting yes.

DON'T FORGET...

You'll find a link to more resources and tools
to build clarity, confidence, and control at
www.RedCapeRevolution.com/BookBonus.

Why the Red Cape Revolution?

Helping you discover simple, practical ways to gain more clarity, confidence, and control in your worklife is at the heart of our work at Red Cape Revolution (*www.RedCapeRevolution.com*).

When we think of true revolutions, we often think of violent, turbulent times. We picture people protesting in the streets, sacrificing to create a new normal inside their society or nation.

Sound exciting? I'm sure to some, especially those who see the possibility of a better future. Sound dangerous? In the Middle East, yes. Here, maybe, if the danger is in killing old assumptions and behaviors.

But this revolution isn't violent. It's passionate. It's persistent. And it's important.

The Red Cape Revolution is important right now because **our working world is crying out for more**—more of our talents, more of our brainpower, more of our energy, more of our hands and legs, more of our caring and love. Yes, love—even in the workplace.

We spend so much time and energy at work, and yet the world still hungers for solutions. The challenges that sit out there are waiting to be solved, and are too important to allow any one of us to sit still, hiding our abilities instead of embracing our superpowers and taking them with us to the office, factory, coffee shop, seat 24B, or wherever we work today.

When you become part of the Red Cape Revolution, you gain the clarity and confidence to find, understand, and share your superpowers in whatever work you do. You take back control, one step at a time, and become your own superhero again. And through this, you start to change the world.

This kind of exciting, transformative change has to happen one person at a time. No company, country, government, or religion can decree it so. **It has to be you.**

Bringing your superpowers to work matters. Wearing your red cape proudly, and feeling clear, confident, and in control makes a difference—not only to you, but to all around you who benefit by your example. You have a gift—or several—that will make a difference not only in your worklife but also in others' lives. It would be a shame to keep that all hidden inside.

So, as you read this book, try the ideas, and practice new actions, remember just one thing. **Remember that it matters—and that the world needs you.**

PART
2

Six Steps to Discovering Your Superpowers

It's now time to gear up, donning the red cape that fits you, and only you. That means discovering your superpowers—the ones you can use to capture more clarity, confidence, and control at work.

Superpowers, you say? Okay, I know. In today's world, hearing the word "superpowers" might first generate images of leotard-wearing nerds at Comic-Con. And that's rarely a pretty sight.

In the Red Cape Revolution, however, your superpowers are a special combination of:

- Your gifts,

- Your passions,

- Your experiences,

- Your attitudes,

- Your abilities,

- Your resources,

- Your relationships,

- Your community,

- Your learnings,

- Your failures,

- Your assets,

- Your special talents, and

- Other powerful stuff about you.

I'm guessing (heck, I know) you have a few of those things, right? Whatever makes up your unique superpowers becomes interwoven in your red cape, helping it catch the air and let you fly through your work and your life.

More Than Just Strengths

Some people have said, "What you're really talking about is strengths, right?" Well, yes…and no. I guess we could think about one element of your superpowers as your strengths. But the reason I don't believe a strengths-focus always works is that when we talk about "strengths," the conversation quickly flips to "weaknesses."

Try it yourself: Ask a friend or colleague to tell you his or her three strengths. Based on my highly unscientific but consistent experience, here's what will happen:

- 72% of people will say something like "Strengths? That's hard. I can (or my spouse/significant other can) sure tell you where I stink, though." (Really. I've had this happen time after time.)

- 24% will hem and haw a minute, look at you twice to make sure you're serious, and then tell you a couple things they t-h-i-n-k they do well.

- The remaining 4% will tell you their strengths. No blush, no stutter, just facts. Good for them.

There's a lot of terrific research done on taking a strengths-based approach to career and personal success, most notably by Marcus Buckingham and Tom Rath. (See their books listed in the Extras at the end of this book, and linked on our page at *www. RedCapeRevolution.com/BookBonus.*)

But even as those authors' research has shown, it's incredibly hard to keep people like you and me—much less our companies and corporations—focused on how to identify and use our strengths, rather than how to default to apologizing and focusing on our weaknesses. There's actually a scientific reason for this. It's called negativity bias. But this isn't a book about science; it's a book about you. Hopefully, as those talented researchers and others like them continue to use their superpowers and help bring a strengths-based focus to their followers, this will change. But for now, most of us still default to what's missing instead of what is.

Where our attention goes, our actions follow. And so if we focus only on strengths, we notice weakness by default.

Not so with superpowers. Let's break it down:

- **Super:** above, elevated. Or great, amazing, superb.

- **Power**: strength, force, focused energy. Granted or taken. Can be used for good or evil.

- **Powers**: special characteristics and talents, i.e., "she has powers of persuasion."

In addition to the actual meaning of the word, having superpowers sounds, well, like FUN! Why wouldn't you want some?

So what's a superpower in today's workplace? Certainly I'm not proposing that we can run faster than a speeding bullet, or that we're able to leap tall buildings in a single bound, right?

Well, if you can run that fast or jump that high, you probably don't need me to help you find your superpowers. But for most of us, our superpowers aren't about just physical extremes, but about our mental, emotional, and spiritual extremes, too.

READY TO GET STARTED?

Go to *www.RedCapeRevolution.com/SuperpowerGenerator* and download our free Superpower Statement Generator with audio coaching to walk you through a simple process to do the work to discover your superpowers. Not online? No worries—there's a version of the Superpower Statement Generator in the Extras section of this book.

Six Steps to Discover Your Superpowers

One thing that's become crystal-clear in all of my work with individuals, teams, and organizations is that **every single one of us has superpowers**—even ones we can't describe or don't yet know. (Honestly, I think many of you actually do know yours; you just don't think it's politically correct to talk about them, much less bring them to work. Time to shake up that belief!)

Discovering your superpowers may hit you like lightning. Or, it may take a little trial and error, like mine did.

But there are some steps you can take to get there faster. What follows are the six I recommend to my clients, audiences, and friends who want to step out into this journey and toward a stronger worklife.

> ### WANT TO SEE HOW I DEFINE MY SUPERPOWERS?
>
> It's in the Extras section at the back of this book, and on our book bonus page at *www.RedCapeRevolution.com/BookBonus.*

Step 1. Listen to the Whispers

"Your life is always speaking to you," said TV's favorite teacher, Oprah Winfrey, as she closed out her 25 years of daytime television. Of all the lessons she's shared over the years, my favorite has been to notice the whispers, the murmurs, the quiet messages that we all have and hear—but don't always notice, or acknowledge.

I heard the whispers for years. At first, they were soft, and the noise in my head easily drowned them out. Then they got louder and louder, and while I tried to cover them up with a busy life, a much-needed books-and-beach weekend with no TV or technology made them show up bigtime. The whispers became screams. And so I had to act.

First, I hired a professional coach. I'd heard of coaching for years, starting with seeing coaching pioneer Cheryl Richardson on TV (now that I think about it, that was on Oprah, too) and reading her first book, *Take Time for Your Life.* But in the real world, I had no idea what a coach really did, nor did I know the right way to choose one. (I do now. I've had a coach—and sometimes more than one—ever since.)

That first coach led me to recognize other whispers I'd been hearing. He helped me get clear about the actions that needed to happen to convert the whispers in my head into the beliefs in my brain, and then the steps to translate the beliefs into words in my mouth.

Then, I did the work. As the saying goes, "wishin' don't make it so." I had to act on the whispers, talk to others about the whispers, answer their questions, answer my questions, and answer the questions the answers raised. It took time, and focus, and energy— all while still living my "normal" life and doing my "normal" work. But I was feeling far from normal.

And that work led me here, to you, and to our little movement to proudly put on our red capes and bring our superpowers to work.

What are your whispers? Take a listen and you may be surprised at what you hear. Oprah and I can't be wrong.

READY FOR A COACH?
Check out the Extras section for resources about where to go and how to choose the right coach for you, or visit *www. RedCapeRevolution.com* to learn how you can work with Darcy.

Step 2. Be Crazy Curious

How often have you heard someone in your office, when faced with a detailed explanation, say "Hey, dude, TMI (too much information). I don't wanna know." But the reality is that knowing more—just a little more—can open up the lucky strikes you're looking for—those flashes of possibility that become part of your superpowers.

How many times do we cut off possibilities and even luck because we stop being curious about the answers (or we think they'll be a waste of time)? My client Kristy, a former management consultant longing for a change, knew she had fun talking and thinking about interior design. But she stopped short of letting herself explore whether design could be a place where she could both have fun and be successful.

Part of our work together involved pushing her to get crazy curious. She started asking herself questions such as:

- Why does this field appeal to me? Is it really about the work of designing, or is it about something else (creativity, freedom, working with people)? If it's something else, do I really know those elements exist in this field, or am I just assuming it does from what I think that life looks like?

- Are other people successful in this field? If they are, how do they get to be successful? If I don't know for sure, who can I ask?

- What other assumptions am I making? What's the real truth there? What do I need to do to confirm or disprove them?

Getting crazy curious is a great way to start clearing some of the underbrush from your path to your superpowers. It opens up the new lanes of possibility and knowledge you haven't traveled down yet—and who knows where that will take you?

Step 3. Know Your Narrative

Let me tell you a story.

Ah, you're paying attention now, right? I see you leaning in, getting ready for what's coming next. It's true—everyone loves a good story.

You are a story yourself, exactly as you are right now. Don't get suckered into thinking you don't have a story—like Meg Ryan in *When Harry Met Sally,* who says, "How can I tell you the story of my life? Nothing's happened to me yet." Wrong.

You have a story. And the key facts from that story are your narrative.

A narrative is your storyline, the clear and simple way you think and talk about yourself. It can become a foundational piece of discovering your superpowers. To really know your narrative, answer two simple questions:

- **What am I known for?** Write down five or six words or phrases—kind of like keywords in a Google search. Resist choosing your title or job description, unless that's really all you're known for (and even then, I'm pretty sure you're not really known just as the "PM for the QA on the ING team." Really.). Make sure you let yourself go beyond your business-y self. In fact, recognizing your most important personal characteristics can often be key to finding the superpowers that help you most at work.

- **What do I want to be known for?** Same exercise, except now step into someone else's shoes. Do your colleagues know you as a great get-it-done guy or gal, but you long to be seen as strategically savvy? Are you always reminding everyone of their commitments and deadlines, but for once, you'd like to *not* be known as the workplace parent?

Pick out the keywords that describe the "who" you want to be.

When you have those words, experiment with putting them together for your narrative. Here are some examples from people I've worked with:

- *Hard-working financial strategist with a soft side for pets.*

- *I'm a cancer survivor bringing that experience to my work as a healthcare consultant.*

- *I bring reliable, smart financial advice sprinkled with my sometimes-hidden creative insights.*

- *Dedicated mom who leads her work teams with the same incredible intuition, structure, and caring she brings to her family.*

- *I'm a fast, creative writer and thinker, developing engaging content and ideas about issues and people who influence the environment.*

What's yours? You don't have to share it with anyone; it's just your own short story, for now. But knowing it will help you get closer to putting on your red cape and bringing your superpowers to work.

Step 4. Sign Your Own Permission Slip

I love Facebook as an inspiration device. Okay, yes, it can become a time-sucker, but I adore how it keeps me connected, provides me with some giggles, and from time to time inspires an idea or two, like the one from my friend Jack, who wrote that he was "signing my own permission slip and taking a field trip."

Now, Jack is what I consider a capital-C Creative—not just playing at it, but actually using his creative superpowers of art and smarts to make his way in the world. He's a unique individual, and one who doesn't need (or likely ask!) anyone's "permission" to do something as innocuous as leaving the office for the day.

But the idea of Jack signing his own permission slip got me thinking. Just like when we were kids and our schools needed signed permission slips to make various radical activities acceptable (like trips to the zoo or the candy factory), you can give yourself permission right now to do the thing you're avoiding, are questioning, or have stalled doing.

Mine would read:

Dear World,

Darcy, as a fully-formed grown-up who can make her own decisions and assess her own consequences, has full consent and permission to do any or all of the following:

- *Daydream for a few hours on a sunny afternoon, even if it is a workday;*

- *Call a colleague she hasn't talked to in a long time without apologizing for not calling sooner (and not feeling guilty, either);*

- *Post a new idea on her blog at www.RedCapeRevolution.com— and not be concerned about how smart the idea is or how well-written the text is, because you have to write the average posts to stumble upon the awesome ones;*

- *Sit an extra 15 minutes after dinner and enjoy the company of those at the table;*

- *Eliminate Internet, newspaper, and TV news for a day and know nothing's really being missed;*

- *Or like Jack, take a day (or just even an hour) to go on a "field trip" in an area of professional or personal interest.*

Signed,
Darcy.

Permission granted!

If there's anything that's getting in the way of listening to the whispers, being crazy curious, or knowing your narrative (the steps we've shared so far), sign your own permission slip and move yourself forward.

What's holding you back from taking the actions you know you need to take on the path to discovering—and using—your superpowers? What do you need to give yourself permission to do/ say/try/ask/propose/risk/fail? Try signing your own permission slip today, and see how much closer it takes you toward finding your own superpower space.

Step 5. Talk to Yourself

A long time ago, in a galaxy far, far away, if we saw someone on the street talking to themselves, we'd s-l-o-w-l-y turn around and head in the opposite direction.

Later in our evolution, we noticed a telltale wire dangling from ear to phone, and in more recent experiences, we've caught a flash of Bluetooth bug in their ear. So we no longer run.

Soon, I am convinced, that bug will be invisible (and may already be by the time you read this). The point here is not to take a stroll down technology memory lane. The point is that you'll no longer be labeled nuts if you start talking to yourself.

So do it. Often. Out loud.

The trick is to **talk nice.** Talk to yourself as if you already have your red cape on. (Remember how that feels? Aren't you standing up straighter, feeling stronger already?) No superhero I know would be telling a great person like you things like:

- "You're going to be stuck in this job the rest of your life, so deal with it."

- "Your boss isn't going anywhere, and so don't expect that promotion."

- "Why should you have a job and a life you love? You're not that special."

In my own journey, I had to start practice talking nice to myself, and I had to stop telling myself things like:

- "I should be aspiring to do anything I can to make more money."

- "I should love this nice job with this nice title at this nice company."

- "I should be happy just as I am."

(As the self-help gurus would say, I was obviously "should-ing" all over myself. Glad that's over.)

When we talk to ourselves over and over again about the things we want, the things we are becoming, and the good things we already are, those words create new connections and patterns in our brains, and, over time, become very, very real.

Talking to yourself isn't crazy. As my grandmother Muz used to say, "Talk to yourself. You'll get all the right answers."

Step 6. Do the Work

In his classic book *The War of Art,* Steven Pressfield puts a name to that mystical, frustrating roadblock that pops up every time we want to do something that's better for us.

He labels it "The Resistance."

And the only way around the resistance is to acknowledge it, make friends with it, and, in the end, do the work (which, not surprisingly, is the name of another great Pressfield book you'll find listed in the Extras section.)

So the sixth step isn't really a big secret. You have to do the work.

Yep, I hear your groans. Hey, if it was easy, everyone would be doing awesome work that's fun for them and useful for others. Problems would be solved. Conflicts would be aligned. Worlds would be at peace.

But they're not. Not everyone has the gumption to do the work.

But you do. I know this because you've already read this far. You're already doing the work. I know you're already hearing the whispers, asking crazy curious questions, knowing your narrative, and signing your permission slips for the next big thing.

Let's make the next chunk of work easy. If you can write a list, you can do this work. And I'll help.

To do the work, try my Superpower Statement Generator at *www. RedCapeRevolution.com/SuperpowerGenerator.* It comes with audio coaching from me, guiding you through each step in the process, where you'll make several lists and sort through those to put together a first stab at your own superpower statement.

Don't get overwhelmed or stuck doing the work. In fact, I often encourage clients to set a timer for 10 minutes for each section, and work furiously for those 10 minutes. When the timer goes off, move on.

There are six sections overall, so if you feel like doing it in one sitting, that's an hour, more or less, plus a few minutes here and there to listen to the accompanying audio coaching. Can you spare an hour in exchange for discovering your superpowers? I think you can. (If you're not sure, think again about what it'd mean to you to have the clarity, confidence, and control that discovering your superpowers will bring.)

IF YOU'RE NOT ONLINE, you can start working through the Superpower Statement Generator on paper in the Extras section of this book.

PART

3

How to Bring Your Superpowers to Work

If you've read this far and have done the work—*especially* if you have done the work—you now have a great idea of what your superpowers are. (I love to hear what you're finding. Come on over and share your discoveries our Facebook page at *www. Facebook.com/RedCapeRevolution*. You might find someone else with similar or parallel powers just waiting out there for you to connect.)

Now it's time to bring those superpowers to work.

If you're like most, that call to action typically stimulates a whole host of questions, like:

- "Can I bring my superpowers to my current work, even if my job/company/boss/industry stinks?"

- "Do I have to find a new job/company/profession/life to use my superpowers? And if I do, how can I possibly do that in this economy?"

- "Can I really make a living when I use my superpowers, or do I have to wear sackcloth and take a pledge of poverty?"

- "What, are you nuts?"

So, some answers:

Yes, you can bring your superpowers to your work right now, exactly where you're currently planted. After all, why wait? Chances are that you picked up this book because you want that elusive clarity, confidence, and/or control, or maybe you're not completely happy with one or more of the following: what you're doing, where you're working, or who you're working with.

You **don't** have to find a new job/company/profession/life to use your superpowers. In talking to my clients, readers, and audience members who've told me their superpower stories, I found:

- About half chose to move on to new opportunities (or to put a plan in place to make a move);

- Half found ways to do things differently right in the job where they are.

Either way, don't get ahead of yourself. Start using your superpowers and staying in your superpower space (more on that in Part 4), and you'll figure out what's right for you.

If you decide it's time to try new work, don't let fears of "the economy" keep you from starting down that path. When it comes to real, meaningful work that makes a difference for people, organizations, and communities, "the economy" is whatever is happening right in front of you.

A Word on "The Economy"

At the time of this writing, U.S. unemployment is over 9%, keeping the media buzzing and talented people hunkering down in jobs they hate, scared to set foot outside their office doors. "Keep your head down," colleagues cry. "You don't want 'the economy' to catch up with you."

But for college-educated, experienced professionals, the unemployment rate is just over 4%, which historically is low. In fact, as many industries are growing and expanding as are shrinking. However, we only hear the slam of the closing doors, not the squeak of the newly opened ones.

There **are** jobs out there, and there are people who want to hire people who bring something special to the table. Don't buy into the myth that they've all gone away.

As an aside, I realize if you're a college-educated professional out-of-work, those numbers are meaningless to you. To you, the unemployment rate is 100%. You're probably already aware that there are plenty of great tools for today's job seeker, but if you'd like additional resources or support, share your search with our community on our Facebook page at www.Facebook/ RedCapeRevolution.com, or link with me on LinkedIn at *www. LinkedIn.com/in/DarcyEikenberg.* You never know who you might connect to, or who may be able to help. Every job opening is a problem to be solved, and who knows—you might be the perfect answer to someone else's problem.

Just know that your biggest challenge in finding a job is the battle of your own mind. Don't let the negative-edged words and emotions around "the economy" talk you out of knowing what your valuable, important superpowers are. Turn off the TV, the blogs, your father-in-law. Talk to yourself. Know your narrative. Sign your own permission slip. Somewhere, there are great people in a great organization who need your gifts desperately. Your job is to keep exploring, talking, and sharing so you can find them and give them what they need.

So for all of us—job holder, job seeker, job changer—remember this. You can make a living—and more importantly, have a life— using your superpowers—whether it's staying right where you are and doing things differently, whether it's creating something different within your same organization, or moving on to another organization, or even creating your own business that demands you bring your superpowers to work every single day. You can do it.

You're a bright professional now armed with clarity, confidence, and control—and our economy needs you.

Six Simple Secrets to Bring Your Superpowers to Work

Here are my secrets you can use to bring your superpowers to work, each and every day. Even though they're simple, they're each powerful and easily put into action. You just have to get started. Pick one and dive in, or try incorporating an idea from each of them. You'll soon see what it feels like to have your red cape flying and your superpowers blazing.

Secret 1: Put the Right Words in Your Mouth

When did "brag" become a four-letter word? It's amazing how even the most articulate and confident people have been brainwashed that bragging is a bad thing, like chewing with your mouth open or belching in public.

But if you don't brag, how will we know all of the unique, special, and amazing things you're doing? How will we notice when you're wearing your (metaphorical) red cape? How will your boss/colleagues/peers/next employer/community/world learn more about you—the best of you—and realize "Hey! It sounds like that gal has an answer to the problem I'm having over here. Let's go talk to her!"?

To bring your superpowers to work, it's time to learn to put the right words in your mouth. **It's time to brag.**

If you're like some in my audiences, you might be shocked at this suggestion. Even the most accomplished, proud, and articulate professionals I work with hesitate here, saying, "I don't want to seem too full of myself." (Wow, I sometimes think when I hear this. What others would give to be as full of talent as you!)

If you're worried about seeming arrogant or cocky, just remember this distinction, from Thomas Leonard, the founder of modern coaching: Confidence is knowing what you do well. Arrogance is covering up what you don't.

Or, as baseball great Dizzy Dean said, "It ain't braggin' if it's true." What's true about you? What are you proud of, excited by, succeeding with? To really bring your superpowers to work, you have to put the right words in your mouth about who you are, what you do, and what you bring to your work and the world. Staying quiet won't cut it.

How to start? One way is take advantage of ongoing situations to turn small talk into big talk. Think about all of the "small talk" situations you've been in at work this week, such as:

- Waiting for everyone to arrive at the meeting (P.S. Using this opportunity should give you more incentive to show up on time, if not early. Be late and miss out!);

- After you've dialed into the conference call and the host is giving the last few stragglers "just another minute";

- Walking to or from the parking lot, lunch room, coffee station, or break area;

- In the elevator; or

- Leaving the bathroom. Not my favorite place to talk, but somehow, people do strike up a conversation!

Each of these times creates a "small talk" opportunity that, with the right words in your mouth, you can make into a "big talk" superpower difference!

Here's a real-life example of how it works. My client Greg worked as a copywriter in a mid-sized advertising agency. After pushing it behind him for a number of years (a bad business school experience did the trick), Greg rediscovered his superpowers of sales and business analysis, skills he wanted to now add to his ad writing ability. He ideally wanted to move into a larger role, developing business for his company, but felt his bosses saw him as "just a writer."

Greg started changing what he was saying in "small talk" situations to better reinforce his business superpowers and create a new, different impression of who he was and what he did. So whenever someone asked the always-present small talk question "How are you?" Greg switched his typical answer of "Fine" to words like:

- "Great! I just noticed our client's sales went up this month. Looks like what we've been creating for their campaign really generated some business."

- "I'm really good, thanks. I was proud to hear that Client X renewed their contract. I know how challenging those negotiations can get and what it takes to close the deal."

- "Great. I'm working on the Client Z account, and starting to do my own research about what's driving their bottom line. It reminds me of a case study we did at Kellogg when I was in B-school. Have you been involved with their business?"

In the course of seconds—really, just seconds—Greg's listener gets the opportunity to learn something totally different about Greg: that he thinks about the business results of campaigns, that he pays attention to the client renewal processes, that he went to a top-level business school, etc. (And as a side note, Greg started to remember how much he enjoyed talking and thinking in this part of his superpower space, and that gave him the confidence to ask for a shot at new responsibilities. He got the chance.)

It worked for Greg because all of these words in his mouth came from a place that was honest, true, and real to him. What you can't read on the page is his tone of voice, his genuine enthusiasm, his pride of sharing these observations and thoughts. His red cape fluttered behind him. When it feels real, it's not bragging.

You may have to experiment for a while to get the right words in your own mouth. Here are some questions to help.

- What's the one project or accomplishment you're most proud of right now? How did your unique superpowers make a difference to the outcome?

- If you weren't worried about what anyone would say or think, what would you want people to know?

- How do you want people to see you in the future? What would you say differently if you started talking as if you were that person right now?

FOR MORE ON THIS TOPIC, I love Peggy Klaus's book, *Brag: The Art of Tooting Your Own Horn Without Blowing It,* which covers the art of bragging in much more depth. You'll find a link at *www.RedCapeRevolution.com/BookBonus.*

Secret 2: Know Who You Need to Know

Almost everything is easier to do when the right people get involved. That goes for bringing your superpowers to work, too. You could do it alone, but why?

If we've learned nothing from the lightning growth of 24/7 communication and social media, it's that people enjoy being connectors and sharing things they like. When you are wearing your red cape and making a difference in your corner of the world, your friends, colleagues, and even casual acquaintances start reinforcing and extending your knowledge, wisdom, and good energy through their words, actions, and thoughts. They spread your superpowers around faster than the latest video of a piano-playing cat.

When more people understand and see your superpowers, you get more opportunities to use them and feel more confident each time you do.

By *knowing* people, I don't mean just listing them in your LinkedIn contacts because you once shared a table at a rubber chicken dinner. I mean *really knowing* people—which requires paying attention to them, asking them questions, being curious and concerned about their well-being. And that takes work, patience, and time. It's easier than ever to have a string of contacts; it's harder than ever to *really know* people, especially the ones you need to know.

Also, let's be clear. Knowing who you need to know is not a Machiavellian scheme to manipulate, impress, or somehow finagle love and appreciation from someone who doesn't want to give it. It's a genuine expression and connection to the people in your work and life world who need—and maybe even want—to know and understand your superpowers, people who can not only gain and benefit but who can help you benefit the world.

41

(Just to say it, the point of this exercise is about building relationships with people who can support you in your superpower space. But some people might consider this activity networking—a word I hate since I am not a tuna and do not want to be caught in your net. There are thousands of books, websites, and blogs about networking if you're interested in this further or need some fresh ideas.)

Roles and relationships are more unpredictable than ever before. Titles and status can mean less than habits and friendships.

So to really bring your superpowers to work, and to live and breathe in your superpower space, who do you need to know? Who needs to know *you*?

If you're my client Greg from the previous example, maybe it's the three top sales executives in his firm, so that he has some real-life role models who are doing what he'd like to do. Maybe it's the person who recently left his company and is now at a competitor.

To bring your specific superpowers to work, think about how it might be helpful to know people like:

- Your biggest competitor,

- Your former boss,

- The peer you never get a chance to talk to,

- The person who got that promotion instead of you,

- The CEO's administrative assistant,

- The vendor liaison,

- The receptionist, guy in the mailroom, or UPS driver,

- Your neighbor's cousin who's looking for a job, or

- Your hair stylist's mom who works in your industry.

How to reach out? Keep it simple, like:

- "I've heard about you from [whatever the source] but don't know much about what you do. Would you be open to having coffee sometime to connect?"

- "I realize we have several [friends/colleagues/business connections] in common but we haven't had the chance to connect. Could we schedule a 15-minute call to get better acquainted?"

- "I've been exploring how I can use my [superpowers, or talents/skills/ideas/energy/resources, for those not cool enough to discover their superpowers yet]. My goal is to make a bigger difference in my work and career, and I'd love to share some ideas with you and hear what's happening with you, too. Would you be willing to get together next week?"

Then make the date, show up, and be your red cape–wearing self. You never know what you'll learn and do when you know who you need to know.

Secret 3: Click Less to Connect More

How many times have you walked into a meeting and noticed everyone with their heads down and fingers flying? This scenario is all-too-familiar in our workplaces, not to mention our homes. And we've accepted it as normal.

In fact, I've heard arguments that our head-bowed, thumb-dancing behavior is the natural extension of our advanced society, that we have to grow up and adapt, and that asking for different behavior is a step backward at best.

To that, I politely say, "Bull."

Yes—our BlackBerrys, iPhones, and other technology tools have changed our lives for the better, arming us with more flexibility, information, and power than ever before.

And—with great power comes great responsibility, as Spiderman says. Even though our use of these tools has exploded with unprecedented speed, no one has stopped to teach us how to integrate them into the work and life we want to have. When there are no rules, the technology rules us.

Letting technology rule might be fine—if everything else was working well. But it isn't. And we're missing something important in our professional and personal lives.

We're missing connection.

"Connection?" you laugh at me, amazed. *"Why, right now I'm connected to my 400 Twitter followers, 875 Facebook friends, and my email contact list in the thousands. I'm more connected than ever before."*

All true. You are connected. But are you connect-*ing*? My clients, friends, and people in my speaking audiences tell me they're not.

In fact, they're feeling:

- *Less* connected to their colleagues, even those just a floor away,

- *More* distant from their friends and family, and

- Even *farther away* from their own thoughts and voices because they're constantly responding to the adrenaline buzz of their device(s).

Connection is a basic human need—a longing, even. We *want* to connect. We know that workplaces where people connect work better, too.

So you'd think we'd do whatever it takes to connect, right? But we're not doing it. In fact, we're unintentionally replacing connecting with clicking.

And it's not working.

The sad part is that I hear people say "that's the way it has to be" to be successful in a wired world. But they're wrong.

It's time to make new rules. Our wonderful technology tools tumbled into our lives with great speed. When we quickly adjusted to integrate their possibilities, we unintentionally created informal, habit-based rules that we never thought through, challenged, or rejected. Until now.

Now, we have the opportunity to design new rules and techniques that work to support our success instead of drain it. With new rules, we can take control of these amazing, empowering tools, take control of our worklives again, and be free to bring our superpowers to work.

If you're ready for new rules, here are four to try. If you want to connect more, try these out and discover how you can click less.

Rule #1: Decide Whether You're Using Your Technology—or Whether It's Using You

Start by asking yourself:

- "Am I 'pulled' into work emails and calls during times I'm trying to be present for my friends or family?"

- "Do my friends or loved ones complain that I pay more attention to the technology than to them?"

- "Do I feel anxious or jumpy when my technology buzzes or beeps?"

- "Do I text or manually dial while I'm driving a car?"

If you've said "yes" to any of these, then your technology is using you. Remember: You're the one with the brains here—and you're too smart to get used.

Rule #2: Experiment with Connecting Differently

In many of our workplaces, it feels like we've forgotten that we have alternatives to email, text, and tweeting. So here's a reminder! You can still:

- Call instead of click. Sure, voicemail can be misused as much as email, but a brief, upbeat, and clear message helps build a stronger personal connection.

- Walk instead of click. Go to someone's location, even if it's a few minutes out of the way. If you're longing for connection, never pass up an opportunity to be face-to-face. It builds relationships, prevents multitasking, generates better ideas, and is just more fun.

- Write instead of click. Physical, handwritten notes are not passé. They're simple to do and carry powerful emotion with them, even when they're just saying a simple "thank you." Notes get saved—and remembered.

Rule # 3: Create Your Click-Free Zones

Your local 7-Eleven® can be open all the time, with a rotating staff in and out. But you, as an individual, can't be "open for business" 24/7—especially if you want to work at your peak energy and be successful.

When your devices are on and you're "open" to receiving and responding to information, you're open for business. But you can choose a time or situation to be "closed," too. I call these your "click-free zones." Here are some my clients have created for themselves.

- On Tuesdays and Thursdays, I don't check email after 7 p.m.

- I do not use my business cell phone on weekends.

- On Mondays, I don't check email until after our weekly staff meeting.

- I don't use my BlackBerry when I'm eating with another person.

Sound extreme? You can make exceptions, as long as they're clear. For example:

- I don't check email after 7 p.m. except during the week we are on deadline with the monthly newsletter.

- I only turn on my iPhone in meetings if I am expecting a client call or we need to find information that will help the meeting. If my iPhone's on for one of these reasons, I'll say so at the start of the meeting; otherwise, it will be off.

Your click-free zone gives you permission to be fully present and attentive at times when you typically aren't. It lets you recharge and refresh, and will strengthen your performance in the long run.

Rule # 4: Share Your Rules With Others

We teach others how to treat us. If we're constantly available and responding—whether or not the request is of high priority and value—we teach them that our time is fully accessible and, as such, less valuable.

Communicate the new rules you've created, and share your click-free zones. Then, act on them consistently. Resist letting others guilt you out of your commitments to yourself.

Resist making too many exceptions, too. They send a message that you aren't really serious, and they make your word less valuable.

Finally, remember that the rules you create are yours and yours alone. They won't work for everyone in the same way you'll make them work for you. You get to give yourself a gift here—to create your rules exclusively for the way you want to work, live, and connect.

Secret 4: Make Uncomfortable Your New Comfortable

We spend a lot of time and money on comfort. We search for the right pillow, the right chair, the right shoes (although my stiletto-wearing friends will disagree with that one).

And yet, many of the best things for us make us uncomfortable: the doctor's visit where we calibrate our health, taking a walk even if we're tired, finishing the taxes tonight instead of waiting until the last minute.

When I bring *my* superpowers to work, it often involves making people uncomfortable. As a leadership and workplace coach, clients hire me to challenge them to take action toward things like building a better work experience, creating stronger career success, or making more meaningful choices about how they use their time and talents. And the only way to do that is to get really, really uncomfortable.

Discomfort is where the growth comes from. As a gardener, I often think about the path the seeds I plant take before they can bloom into amazing flowers. First, they're buried in the cold, dark ground. On their own, they crack open their shells, push through the hard dirt, and s-t-r-e-t-c-h higher toward the sun and the light. They also fight off the squirrels and survive on minimal water when I forget to drag the hose over. And yet, they bloom into something gorgeous.

That process can't be comfortable. So even if it feels like you're planted in the dirt for now, know that you don't have to be standing still, rotting. You stand tall, knowing that your discomfort shows you're growing—and pushes you to reach for the sunshine.

If you're someone who wants to keep growing and sprouting new leaves in your work or life, it's time to make uncomfortable your new comfortable.

49

Are you ready to make uncomfortable your new comfortable? If so, here are three ways to do it.

1. Notice Your Comfort Catches

We can't create discomfort if we keep deferring to our comfort routines. Do you opt for silence in disorganized team meetings instead of asking "Guys, how can we get more organized?" Do you stay in the same job or career because others have said you've "got it great"?

What's your comfort catch? Notice the times when you long for change, but hear yourself saying "Yes, but...." Your "buts" are great clues that you're in a comfort catch.

Our comfort routines are there because they keep us warm and safe, which is a lovely place to be—for a while. But as the old saying goes, "A ship in port is safe—but that's not what ships are for." What's waiting inside you, ready to launch? The world is waiting for you to set sail.

2. Build the Discomfort Muscle

What's the one thing you could do to make yourself really *uncomfortable* today—but could open up new paths toward better outcomes, greater possibilities, and getting what you want? When I asked some of my clients this question, they said things like:

- Tell my boss I disagree with her decision, and why.

- Keep my BlackBerry turned off all morning so I can plan this afternoon's meeting.

- Say no to being on the volunteer team.

What's yours?

3. Affirm the Squirm

When you build a physical muscle, it's inevitable you'll sweat. When we're building a mental muscle, we squirm. We wriggle and twist and feel out of place.

To make uncomfortable your new comfortable, I say affirm the squirm. Know that your discomfort is just a signal—one that helps you recognize it for what it is, but isn't enough to make you give in, or go backward.

So when you start feeling antsy, try having a little chat with yourself (remember: talking to yourself is good!) that can go something like this:

> "Ah, yes, there you are, squirmy feelings. I've been expecting you to pop up soon! Nice of you to visit while I'm challenging myself to do something different. Thanks for stopping by. You can go now."

The squirm confirms you're moving out of your comfort zone. That's good—that's progress.

Secret 5: Build Your Support Team

When I led a regional division of a large HR consulting firm, Bridget was my boss Suzanne's executive assistant. Even though we worked 500 miles apart, it was easy to see how she kept Suzanne moving quickly and efficiently through the quagmire of work, deadlines, and details a senior corporate leader has to face. And she did it with a smile.

One day, Bridget called me. Her husband was being transferred to my city and she wondered if I would be open to her transferring into the group I led there. Would I!

I immediately said yes to put her mind at ease and prevent any thoughts of her searching for work elsewhere. Then I realized we had no open assistant positions at the time, and certainly none at the level of Bridget's expertise.

So I called Suzanne to discuss it. I had mapped out various creative ways to share Bridget's talent locally with other departments and teams, and knew Suzanne would support anything to keep Bridget at our company. I started to spin what I thought were practical solutions, when Suzanne interrupted me and said, "Darcy, just have Bridget support you directly. She'll take things off your plate you haven't even thought of yet. With her support, you'll be able to do so much more than you can right now."

It was a lesson that changed my worklife. It made me change my mental definition of the word "support" from "a way to get help" to "a way to build you up." I had been caught up in the minutia of "how" and "when," and my big-picture-thinking boss was focused on the "why"—why more support would be good for me and our business. As a byproduct, of course, the "why" was also good for Suzanne, since she could keep an excellent employee (Bridget) and increase the contributions of another (me).

And Suzanne's prediction came true: With Bridget's support, I was able to focus more on higher-value activities that made a bigger difference to our people, clients, and business—work that I now know was much closer to my superpower space.

Bridget taught me how important getting the right support was, and now, long after I've left that job and she's retired from that company, she still does. Even though I need a reminder now and then, I know for sure that building your support team is essential to bringing your superpowers to work.

How Can I Build My Support Team?

Not everyone can be lucky enough to have a Bridget in their lives. But it's easier than ever today to seek out the support you need in all areas of your work and career.

Maybe you don't have a Suzanne who can give you the assistant of your dreams, but what's the support you can ask for at work? If you're in a role working with a professional administrative assistant, are you asking enough of him or her? A true admin pro wants to be involved, proactive, and part of the solution, but sometimes finds he or she is only getting the request to execute. Do you really understand his or her superpowers, and how you can use them? (Have you even asked? Try: "Hey, I know we both really want to do great work here. Is there a better way we could be using your abilities that helps us all move forward?")

Maybe you need to make a business case for additional assistant support, whether as an employee or a contractor. (The growing world of virtual assistants makes it easier than ever to do this.) I'm always amazed at the companies that see assistants as a cost and not an asset.

For example, I was hired to lead coaching groups for selected high-potential employees at a major technology firm. For me, the best part of these groups was watching talented, insightful people actively growing their own leadership skills as well as supporting each other in the day-to-day challenges of a fast-paced environment. The worst part of these groups was that these busy, high-performing (and highly paid) people did not have administrative support and so had to schedule the groups themselves, juggling six busy internal calendars and one outsider's (me). If you've ever scheduled a meeting in a large organization with multiple people, you know that even with great calendaring technology this isn't a simple task. If you broke down their salaries into hourly rates, I shudder to think what that deceptively simple task was costing that company.

Another way to build your support team is to ask. Are there others in your company who you can swap superpowers with? Maybe you can work on their spreadsheets if they'll help you with your stand-up presentations. Or are there others in your industry you can mastermind or brainstorm with to find better solutions to your workplace problems? It's easier than ever to meet people like this at professional associations or to post questions in online groups such as LinkedIn.

What's the support you need to really be your best in your superpower space? Your red cape doesn't get hung by the door when you get home; it's part of you. Beyond your workplace, start to think about your support team more broadly:

- Do you need a new doctor, nutritionist, massage therapist, or workout buddy to help you feel better?

- Is it time to see an image consultant, personal shopper, or hair stylist so you can look better?

- Would a personal organizer, housekeeper, tax accountant, or lawn service eliminate some stress so you can think better?

- How would a coach, mastermind group, or community college class help you just **be** better?

Finally, if you're saying right now, "I'd love more support, but can't afford it," you're not alone. But you're wrong. Here's why.

Everything we do either costs us energy or gives us energy. Activities outside our superpower space always *cost* us energy; we notice them by calling them "draining," "exhausting," or "overwhelming." Work in our superpower space *gives* us energy, even if the work is complex and hard. If it's the right work, you can be tired at the end of a day, but still feel excited, proud, and energized.

Money is just an exchange of energy. Paying it to someone to eliminate the energy drains around you—the things that aren't in your superpower space but might be in someone else's—can be the best investment in yourself you'll make. What's it worth to you to be in your superpower space, feeling proud and great, more often?

Here's my own example. I am really, really clear about my superpowers, and keeping an organized space is not one of them. My brain is very organized; my physical environment, well, not so much. Intellectually, I know I *can* clean a closet; I know how and am bodily able. Yet, the idea of spending precious time doing it bores and drains me, and so I procrastinate, make half-hearted attempts on rainy days, and end up spending more brainpower avoiding the job than doing it.

Until I met Emily. Emily is a certified professional organizer, and she's in her superpower space doing the same exact things that rob me of mine. Plus, since she cleans and rearranges closets, drawers, and secret stashes all the time, she does it quickly and efficiently, and she knows the tricks and tools to get the job done. I might wander in the Container Store for hours; Emily knows what's there before she goes.

I first hired Emily to organize my small yet cluttered kitchen. Then my office. Then a closet. And another. What I've gained in time, refreshed energy, less guilt on those rainy days, and better use and enjoyment of my physical environment has been worth every penny of my investment in her superpowers.

What support do you need right now to be able to bring your superpowers to work each and every day, to feel clear, confident, and in control? What would it be worth to you to feel like that? It's easier than you think—so start building that support team now.

FOR MORE RESOURCES, check out the lists in the "Extras" section at the end of this book, or visit *www.RedCapeRevolution.com/BookBonus.*

Secret 6: Get Some Rest

This point usually surprises most people, who think that bringing your superpowers to work means being all hard-charging and activity-filled. But if you want to wear your red cape and soar through your work and life, no matter what your superpowers are, I say you need to get some rest.

Rest is not luxury anymore. There's definitive neurological research (that means brain, people) that proves how working with less than five hours of sleep a night is actually as diminished as if you were driving under the influence of cocktails. Other research is starting to show how lack of rest will not only cause distraction, which can be dangerous, but can also start to cause brain damage.

I was reminded about the importance of rest when reading an article on the 2010 Colgan Air crash that killed 50 people. While several issues appeared to come into play to create this tragedy, the one that kept popping up was the issue of pilot fatigue, or not enough rest.

The Wall Street Journal quoted a memo from Colgan management to pilots stating "frivolous [fatigue] calls are now the majority." The article said the memo "concluded that 'blatant abuse' of time-off requests 'at the expense of our customers and our operational reliability is not an acceptable practice,' and will prompt speedy disciplinary action." So, it's like your mom saying "Don't tell me you're tired. Clean your room, or else!"

So what's a gal (or pilot?) to do? Are our employers able to determine whether we're really tired—or if we're being lazy? Every workplace wants its people to show up bright-eyed and sharp, but can we assess exhaustion versus incompetence? What's more, do we have the sensitivity to ask, or the patience to find out? We have to know and decide what's right for us.

Thankfully, no one will get injured when I'm tired in my workplace. But it makes me less creative, less prolific, and contribute less value to my clients, audiences, and community. That in itself says it's time for a rest.

Contrary to how we're living these days, human beings are not computers. We can't run 24/7. (I'm not even sure my computer can do that; it gets all hot and cranky, too.) It's easy to think we can push a little more, get up a little earlier, work a little later. We tell ourselves we'll catch up on the weekends, on vacation, when we retire. Right.

Author and researcher Tony Schwartz offers great insights about these attitudes based on his work with high-end sports performers as well as corporate execs. Tony teaches that we tend to live our lives as a marathon, when our bodies and minds are actually built for sprints. We perform best when we go all out and focused for a short period of time, have a break or rest, and then go all out and focused again. And, instead of wasting time, this strategy makes us more focused and productive.

Tony says that he wrote his book *How to Be Excellent at Anything* in less than half the time than his previous book because he used sprints and rest instead of treating the book as a marathon.

Ways to Get More Rest

So, are you getting enough rest? If you're like most in my audiences when I ask this question, you quietly smile and shake your head. "I've got four kids," one woman in Nashville said. "Rest isn't an option for me."

I'm going to disagree. In fact, for that Music City mom, I think rest is even more important than ever. Notice that I didn't say "get more sleep," which we often hear (and write off as a platitude just like "eat healthy" and "exercise more"—all true but easier said than done). Sleep is important, and there's tons of great content written about how to get a better night's sleep. (One of my tools is to keep a playlist of sleep meditations and lyric-free music on my iPod to settle an overworked brain.)

In my experience, sleep can be elusive and hard to do in the middle of the day for most corporate types. But rest can be planned.

If you want to bring your superpowers to work, I challenge you to find those little spaces in your day where you can get some rest, in a way that's restful to you, such as:

- My friend John, who sits in his car after lunch and spends 10 minutes listening to loud rock-and-roll.

- My client Amy, who plans an extra 15 minutes for any meeting on the other side of her work campus so she can walk outside on her way back.

- My friend Nick, who takes a seat in the lunchroom nearest the window to watch the birds visit the feeder.

- My former colleague (who shall remain nameless) who uses the bathroom in the lobby instead of using the facilities on her floor so that she has a reason to walk the stairs a few times a day, breathe a little deeper, and collect her thoughts along the way.

What's the way that *you* get some rest? What actions hit your restart button when your energy is low? Work those little moments—those brief segments—into your day. It can be as easy as setting a timer for one minute and closing your eyes. Try it yourself. A minute can actually be a mighty long time.

So those are the six simple secrets to bring your superpowers to work:

1. **Put the Right Words in Your Mouth**

2. **Know Who You Need to Know**

3. **Click Less to Connect More**

4. **Make Uncomfortable Your New Comfortable**

5. **Build Your Support Team**

6. **Get Some Rest**

In the next chapter, we'll talk about the next stage: how to stay in your superpower space, no matter what.

HAVE QUESTIONS OR COMMENTS?

Share them on our Facebook page at *www.Facebook.com/ RedCapeRevolution,* or email us at *info@RedCapeRevolution.com.*

PART
4

Staying in Your Superpower Space

At this point, you've hopefully made good progress on the journey outlined in this book.

- You understand the ideas behind the Red Cape Revolution, and why we need your participation in it now more than ever;

- You see how wearing your own red cape at work can help you start soaring, and you recognize how knowing your superpowers can bring you clarity, confidence, and control;

- You've started doing the work to discover your superpowers; and

- You've put your superpowers to work, in whatever work you're doing or aspire to be doing.

Congrats on traveling this far. It's farther than most will ever get. Most will settle for comfortable (there's that word again), ordinary, and average. But that's not you. Take a minute to appreciate and acknowledge yourself for having the guts to challenge yourself and to get this far.

[Loud screaming applause.]

At this point, you can go farther. I've seen it—I know it.

And, you may slip back. I've seen that, too. Have worn the t-shirt myself.

This section is all about keeping on track, staying and playing in your superpower space, making it an undeniable part of you that you couldn't change even if you tried. It's about continuing on the path you started down—the path you may have been traveling even before you picked up this book.

I'll share some common things that happen that make us forget about wearing our red cape, along with simple, practical ways to shake the wrinkles out and start soaring once again.

How Do You Know if You're Off Track?

Like any newly created path, the first few steps might be well-trampled and clear to follow. But it's likely that you'll arrive at a place where you'll need to dig out some of the underbrush or throw down some more mulch when the path seems to fade into the woods. It's good to know that now, so that when the path is harder to see, you're expecting it—and you have your shovel handy.

So how will you know if you're getting off track? Here are some of the key behavioral indicators (or, said more simply, stuff you say and do) I've found:

You know you're NOT in your Superpower Space when...	You know you're in your Superpower Space when...
Getting up and going to work is hard. You feel exhausted most mornings, and Sunday evenings feel depressing.	Getting up and going to work is easy. You still might need a few more zzz's, but you're not dreading the morning.
The day passes s-l-o-w-l-y.	The day flies by.
Several things on your to-do list make you grimace.	Several things on your to-do list make you grin.
Nothing on your to-do list makes you grin.	Nothing on your to-do list makes you go "yuck."
There are things on your to-do list that have been on there f-o-r-e-v-e-r, that you just can't seem to get around to completing.	Nothing on your to-do list has been there f-o-r-e-v-e-r, postponed, and procrastinated. It's all pretty fresh, interesting stuff.
There's no time in your schedule to think, connect, and breathe. Eating lunch and going to the bathroom are luxuries.	You've got some white space in your schedule to think, connect, and breathe. Of course you eat lunch and go to the bathroom when you need to—you're human, aren't you?
You're tied to your BlackBerry, iPhone, or device of choice, and you respond to its every beepy demand, no matter what you're doing, who you're with, or what time of day it is.	You're using your BlackBerry, iPhone, or device of choice to do what you need, when you need it. You're not letting it—and others through it—use you.
By the end of the week, nothing's changed.	By the end of the week, you know you've done at least one thing that's made a difference for yourself or someone else.
By the end of the week, you haven't grown.	By the end of the week, you've pushed and challenged yourself and/or others just a little, testing your superpowers even more.
The people most important to you complain they never see you, don't know what's happening with you, and are not sure you care.	The people most important to you still know who you are—and like you anyway.

Stop for a minute and think about your own specific superpowers. What are the key behavioral indicators that let you know when you're in—or veering out of—your superpower space?

Here are a few real-world examples from my clients and participants in my speaking and workshop events. As you are reading them, remember: each of these is specific to that person's own superpowers, workplaces, and particular challenges.

I'll know I'm NOT in my Superpower Space when...	I'll know I AM in my Superpower Space when...
I take on new assignments presented in the staff meeting without having a broader conversation with my boss and colleagues about both my capacity and where the work can get done best.	I don't automatically agree to take on the new assignment presented in the staff meeting.
I avoid having a conversation with my district manager about doing something different.	I have the conversation with the district manager about creating the new role I've designed that will help our business and that I'll love.
I get mad when a colleague gets a promotion I thought I deserved.	I have the guts to ask specifically why I did not get the promotion, the openness to hear it, and the ability to decide for myself what I want to do with that information.
I'm so tired I snap at my mom when she calls.	I am focused enough to remember to call my mom once a week because I know it's important to her to hear from me.
I hear myself talking about finding a new job but never do anything about it.	I am setting up short meetings with colleagues in my industry and getting curious about what else is out there.
I'm constantly feeling scared that I'm going to lose my job.	I'm doing the work now on my financial foundation, professional skills, and personal resilience that will give me confidence and control if I should happen to lose my job or want to choose to leave it.

Even without knowing who these people are and what superpowers they're bringing, you can see how situation-specific indicators can be useful. They make it real and help you not fall back into habits that keep you in the past, out of your superpower space.

Have a few ideas for your own behavioral indicators? Make the list now.

Remember, here's the structure:

I'll know I'm NOT in my Superpower Space when…	I'll know I AM in my Superpower Space when…

Say them out loud a few times. Put them on a sticky note on your computer or your dashboard. Set a calendar reminder for them once a day so they pop up on your mobile device. Once you've identified them clearly (there's that benefit of clarity again!), you'll be quick to notice them and re-adjust or celebrate as needed!

Five Ways to Get Back on Track

Have you caught yourself getting off track, stepping backward into your pre–Red Cape Revolutionary days? Do you feel overwhelmed, crazy busy, and unsure what to do when there's so much to do? Have you noticed you're racing with the rats again, instead of using your more evolved levels of mammalian intelligence, emotion, and skill?

Okay, breathe. It will be okay. You can get back on track.

When you catch yourself sliding backward instead of soaring upward, it's tme to shift direction. Here are my five favorite ways to help you get back on track and stay in your superpower space.

1. Drop the Ball

Imagine playing catch with your daughter, getting a nice rhythm of toss and catch going. Then your son pitches a ball your way, your spouse throws another, your neighbor another, your mailman one more. They keep coming faster, and faster, and—OUCH!

You can't catch all those balls. You also can't throw them back quick enough. And when you're trying to catch them all, the valuable experience with your daughter disappears.

We wouldn't think about catching all of those balls in the backyard. So why do we try to catch them all at work? My challenge to you is to start dropping one—or many—right now.

Yes, I see you quiver. If that thought makes you uncomfortable (there's that word again!), well, you're not alone. It's counter-cultural today to think about **not** doing something; we've been taught that the key to success is to do, do, do. But that, my friends, is a lie, lie, lie.

As I've said before, people are not computers. We cannot just add a new memory chip, or upgrade to higher bandwidth. If you're constantly expanding your capacity to catch and handle all the balls coming your way—especially balls that aren't making the most of your talents and your superpowers—you're kidding yourself. You're actually diminishing your own resources, not expanding them—and that's not helping your company or your career.

In fact, it's a myth to think that your work speaks for itself, and that taking more work equals more good buzz about you. Taking more work on that's not in your superpower space wears you down and isn't a career growth strategy; it's a recipe for failure.

If you can't imagine letting a ball sit on the floor, untouched, remember that catching all the balls will not only spell failure for you, but also for your organization. **When there's no pain**—when there are no balls rolling on the ground, with no one to handle them—**it's harder to notice what problems need to be solved.** When you're catching all the balls, it's not as obvious to your organization's leaders that it's time to hire, eliminate outdated processes or systems, change or create a role, or even reward your or other people's contributions. You are letting your own system absorb the shock rather than sharing it with the system that is the organization.

Catch the balls that make sense for you—the ones where you can wear your red cape and bring your superpowers to work. Let the others bounce off your chest confidently and roll onto the ground. Try dropping some balls—and holding tight to the few that matter most.

2. Cut the Waste

In most companies, the "people part" of the business is still called human resources. You (the human) are a vital, important resource to the organization—a resource to be invested and "spent" just like money, energy, and time.

When you're doing the wrong work—especially work that is not in your superpower space—you're actually wasting the company's resources, whether you work for a Fortune 500 business or a four-person shop. And who doesn't hate waste?

To get back in your superpower space, examine everything you're doing, then take each item and ask yourself:

- "Is this the most important thing I can contribute to our business right now? If not, does it even need to be done? If it needs to be done, does it need to be done now?"

- "Given my superpowers and ways I can contribute best, is doing this the best use of my time and talents?"

- "If I were paid an hourly rate for this work, would it be worth it?" (Not sure of your hourly rate? Divide your weekly pay by the number of hours you typically work each week.)

See some waste in your worklife? Try having a very real and business-centered conversation with your manager or leader. It might sound something like this:

- "I'm concerned we're wasting company resources to have this action on my list when I could be investing more time in [higher value work that makes the most of your superpowers and a greater difference to the organization]. Can we brainstorm how to get this done by a lower-cost resource or whether our business needs us to do it at all?"

- "I know you want me to focus on [whatever you've agreed your goals are]. So to do that, I've noticed I need to stop doing [the wasteful thing]. Is it still important, and if so, how do you want me to hand it off?"

- Or, someone at my client whose high potential leaders were asked to do their own scheduling of meetings could say, "We seem to be spending a lot of time back-and-forth managing complex schedules—time I'd like to see pointed toward our product development instead. I bet there are enough small tasks like this around that could help us make more of our top talent's time and make even one part-time assistant pay for him or herself. How could we do that?"

Eliminating hidden waste is one of the biggest business improvement opportunities for organizations today. By cutting the waste, both you and the company win.

A Side Note on Waste: From Status Quo to Status Go

If you're like many of my clients, you're interested in ideas like the Red Cape Revolution exactly because you see the waste and bureaucratic processes within your own organizations. And you don't think it'll ever change.

I'm not naïve. I've lived in the bellies of competitive, high-performing organizations, as an employee, as a manager, as an executive, and as an outside coach and consultant working in the heart of the environment. I know what's still happening in even the most enlightened of organizations. Seemingly strong and confident people resort to cover-your-ass-ets behavior. Meetings are managed mindlessly and mistakenly. New reports emerge to report on reports.

And even though you know it's a waste, you know it doesn't add value, you know your superpower is not linked to how many people you cc on your email, you do it anyway.

Each one of these wasteful decisions are just habits—ones that have been accepted and institutionalized because no one like you has been clear enough, confident enough, and in control enough to take actions to move the status quo to status go.

Take a look at this list of real-life habits and ideas from my clients and colleagues that were switched to less-wasteful alternatives—and all without a lot of pain and agony.

Status Quo Habit	Status Go Alternative
Take five hours each month to put last month's sales data in Powerpoint. Email that 250MB document to the each member of the sales team, who may never even open it since they're out of the office with customers, and likely won't adjust any behavior based on it.	Lead a 15-minute informal call, recorded for playback later for those who can't attend, sharing the highlights of the monthly sales results and giving two or three areas of focus for the sales team this month.
Attend a weekly 60-minute meeting, even though there's no clear agenda and no particular need for your expertise.	If the meeting seems of little value, versus the value of team time spent, suggest to the leader that "the weekly meeting isn't needed anymore." Suggest a less-frequent schedule or reason to eliminate it entirely, giving freedom to call a new meeting on specific topics when needed. If the meeting seems of value to some, let the leader know you observe you're no longer needed, and that you'll schedule a 10-minute check-in with him or her the day after the meeting to see if anything needing your attention emerged.
Copy everyone on email discussions aimed at resolving an issue, just to make sure all involved know what's happening and no one feels left out.	Send one email outlining the process to resolve the issue ("Rather than continuing to debate this in email, Dave, Sandy and I will meet and resolve it. If you feel you need to be part of that discussion, let me know by tomorrow.") Take the discussion off-line (or at a minimum, start a fresh email chain). Send a new email to the interested parties when the issue is resolved.

3. Lose the Guilt

Everyone I have worked with has probably heard me say that human beings are messy. And I mean that with love; messy is good, messy is interesting, messy is creative.

Because we're so creative (yes, even you actuaries who say you're not), we constantly think of new actions and ideas that can move ourselves and our work forward.

Ideas are good. But too many ideas start to pile up and make "good" feel overwhelming, and cause us to get distracted, move away from our true superpowers, and try to tackle more and more of those ideas. And we have the very real and human emotion of guilt when we can't do it all.

Guilt, one ethicist wrote, is to the soul as pain is to the body—a wake-up call, a signal that something needs attention. In my work, I've found that the guilt can get pretty strong when we're out of sync with our superpower space, when we're missing the clarity, confidence, and control we long for.

Consider this your permission to lose the guilt. (Need a permission slip? You know how to do that now, too—or go back and read Part 2 again.) You are highly capable of doing many things, but the most important work is that which is in your superpower space.

Remember that just because you *can* do something, doesn't mean you *should*. I can reorganize my kitchen, but hiring the professional organizer to do it lets me spend that time in my superpower space—and she in hers. (For more on this, see "Build Your Support Network" in Part 3). If the activity you're engaged in is not something making the best use of your superpowers, find another solution. They're out there.

When you're working in your superpowers and doing your best work that matters, there's nothing to be guilty about. We can experience less guilt because our soul has less to complain about.

We're more sure than ever we're doing the right things.

Still feel like you should hold a little guilt? Okay. Feel guilty if you're not bringing your gifts to the world—because there's someone out there who really needs what you have to offer. And how dare you deprive the world?

4. Be the Love

Sometimes the reminders of how to stay in your superpower space can come from the most unusual places.

Case in point: I had a big meeting with a new client company on Valentine's Day one year. (We didn't plan it that way; it was just another workday.) When I arrived, the receptionist's desk was filled with flowers, chocolates, and packages waiting to be delivered throughout the facility, all potential expressions of someone's love for some employee there.

It occurred to me that we don't have any problem bringing the chocolate or the roses into our workplaces—but what about the love? Doesn't seem to be a lot of room for that.

It seems like we decided to treat "love" as a four-letter word at work. "Nothing to love here," said an overworked former colleague with thumbs-a-flying on his BlackBerry. "All I love is getting out of here at 6," said another friend.

Later that same Valentine's Day, I had drinks with a private client of mine who was truly soaring through her work. She'd just earned industry honors and gotten a raise, and really felt centered in her superpower space. And a year earlier, she was ready to quit. How things can change!

I told her my story about seeing all the roses and chocolates, and shared my thought about the absence of love at work. She told me, "Darcy, I never worry about that. In my office, I am the love." And in looking at her smile, I knew that was true.

My client is the exception right now. How did we manage to practically eliminate one of the most positive, forward-moving emotions from our workplaces? How did we get to be afraid of love? Emotion, after all, is what causes motion. Love brings positive, productive motion; fear just keeps moving us backward.

So, as my valentine to you—no matter what time of year you're reading this—I offer you one of the most powerful ways you can stay in your superpower space, all the time, anywhere, no matter what. Just be the love.

Love the people you're with. Make time each day to connect with at least one person, whether it's a hallway hello or a quick smile via instant message. Pay attention to their superpowers and help them along. (You can give them a copy of this book, or send them a link to our blog at *www.RedCapeRevolution.com*.) Our experience at work is greatly influenced by our experience with others, so adding more love to your day-to-day experiences will rub off on your experience with your work.

Extend your love even to the annoying people, the haters, the slackers. A tip that always works for me is to exchange my frustration for empathy. So, instead of "Grrr—David is so annoying," I switch my response to "Hmm—I'm so fortunate I don't approach life like David does." David gets a healthy dose of my empathy and even love—and he doesn't even know it.

Love the environment you're in. Sick of your taupe corporate workspace? How can you change it? I once took an old piece of Hawaiian shirt fabric and tucked it under the acoustic tiles in my ceiling (you know, those things you toss the pencils up into?). In minutes, I had a colorful curtain of "wallpaper" with no muss or fuss—and without incurring the wrath of the office space manager. Spend lots of time in the car? Add a pillow to your seat, a six-pack of water, or some fun audiobooks for the ride. No matter where you work, there are little things you can do to love your space more.

And finally, love the work you do. After all, this is the ultimate goal of staying in your superpower space, right? What you do when you bring your superpowers to work matters more than ever, making more of a difference for your company, community, and your world. We spend a lot of time in work mode, so why not love all of it?

5. Remember Why it Matters

Why put yourself through this, anyway—all this rigmarole about capes and superpowers and soaring and stuff? Why can't you go back to how it used to be, even if what used to be wasn't so hot? Why isn't the "same as usual" good enough?

When you get off track from working in your superpower space—when things seem more challenging, more time-consuming, or more emotional than ever before—just remember one thing. Remember why it matters.

You read why it matters at the beginning of this book. We've got a universe full of problems to solve, and some of them are calling to you, needing you desperately. Putting on your red cape and bringing your superpowers to work can matter to your colleagues, companies, and communities, and to our world. And it will matter to you.

You have a gift—or many—that will make a difference not only in your worklife but also in others' lives. There's no time to be selfish; no time to keep that all hidden inside. So remember why it matters. We need you.

The Big Finish—
Or Maybe Just the Start

You probably picked up this book for a specific reason. Maybe it was to find ways to advance your job or your career. Maybe it was because your organization is changing, and you want to keep up. Maybe you just liked the idea of finding more clarity, confidence, and control.

No matter why you came, I hope you found something of value here. My great wish is that:

- If you were stuck, you now have the clarity you need to walk out of the mud.

- If you thought you had something different or more to give in your worklife, you now are confident that you're right.

- If you were worried that it was hard, you learned how you can take control to make it simple (or at least, simpler than you thought).

I hope these ideas have given you power over the fear and uncertainty that permeate almost every facet of our work environment today. I know you have the talent and energy to move forward with all the clarity, confidence, and control you need. I know you're ready to put on your red cape and bring your superpowers to work.

But please don't delay—the world is waiting.

DON'T FORGET to take advantage of all of the tools, links, and additional ideas on our bonus page at *www.RedCapeRevolution. com/BookBonus*. We're updating tools there and on the site www.RedCapeRevolution.com all the time, so keep checking back.

Extras

Want more? Good, because we have more!

This Extras section has these major components:

- *Your Superpower Statement Generator* (also available online with audio coaching at *www.RedCapeRevolution.com/ SuperpowerGenerator);*

- *What to Say to Build Confidence*—a list of words and phrases you can use in different situations;

- *Questions to Create Conversations* that you can use to talk to others about this book;

- *A Message for Managers and Leaders: Ten Things Your People Want*—for those of you who play these roles in your worklife;

- *Darcy's Story & Superpower Statement,* if you're curious to learn more about me;

- *References & Resources,* so you can discover more great material from fantastic authors who've inspired me;

- *Talk to Us*—how to share more with the Red Cape Revolution team; and

- *About Red Cape Revolution.*

Plus, if this Extras section isn't enough for you, don't forget there's loads of other info, plus links to all of these resources at *www. RedCapeRevolution.com/BookBonus.*

In addition, don't forget that one of the biggest Extras of all is that you now get what it means to be part of the Red Cape Revolution. To keep the momentum going, make sure you're signed up at *www. RedCapeRevolution.com* to receive our twice-monthly Community News for ongoing ideas and inspiration, and check in with us on our Facebook page (*www.Facebook.com/RedCapeRevolution*).

Your Superpower Statement Generator

The simplest way to use our Superpower Statement Generator is to get it online at *www.RedCapeRevolution.com/SuperpowerGenerator*. When you go online, you'll also be able to access audio coaching from me to help you through the process all along the way.

But, maybe you're reading this somewhere unplugged, whether by choice or chance. If that's the case, then use these pages to get started.

By the end of this work, you'll have built one or two statements you can use to talk about the superpowers you bring to work—and to the world.

If you struggle a little—hey, you're normal! Most of us are never encouraged to shout out all the unique and special things about ourselves, so writing them down may feel a bit odd. But if it helps, **you are officially given permission by proclamation of the Red Cape Revolution to let your ego go wild here**. Be honest about how great you are.

Also, your final statements may not feel perfect right off the bat. That's okay. Keep looking at them. Set them aside, and pick them up later. No matter what, after going through these steps, you'll be a lot closer to describing what's unique, special, and important about you.

Ready to get started? Let's go!

Step 1: Build the Base

Let's start from the ground up. On the next page, list 10 of your talents and skills, and 10 awesome gifts you bring to the world. Yes, you have 10 of each—at least!

If you get stuck, set a timer for 10 minutes and **don't stop writing** until the bell rings. (If you come up with more, please add more rows and grow the list. The larger the base, the more superpower fuel for you.)

When you have 10 in each column, put an X next to five of your faves—the ones you love using, the ones you're most proud of, anything that strikes you as your favorite. You'll have five X's in total (not five per column).

My Talents & Skills	Fave 5	My Awesome Gifts	Fave 5
Example: I'm detail-oriented.		*Example: I laugh easily.*	X
Example: I solve problems quickly.	X	*Example: Writing comes easily to me.*	
1.			
2.			
3.			
4.			
5.			
6.			
7.			
8.			
9.			
10.			

Step 2: Add Your Layers

You're more like an onion than a potato: you have lots of layers. So now, let's add other aspects of you, including your attitudes and approaches (how you see things, etc.) and your reachouts and resources (people, groups, and/or relationships you have that can contribute to your success).

Just like before, mark your Favorite 5.

My Attitudes & Approaches	Fave 5	My Reachouts & Resources	Fave 5
Example: I'm extremely kind.	X	*Example: Dad is a financial wizard.*	
Example: I get impatient to fix problems.		*Example: I have 475 LinkedIn contacts.*	X
1.			
2.			
3.			
4.			
5.			
6.			
7.			
8.			
9.			
10.			

Step 3: Other Powerful Stuff About You

Something still missing? What else is really important and powerful about you? Don't second-guess yourself if you have an inkling; trust your gut and write it down. Then, is it a fave? (Psst.... If it's coming up now, chances are it's pretty powerful and deserves an X.)

Other Powerful Stuff	A Fave
Example: My cancer scare taught me to be more sensitive to others' stresses.	X
1.	
2.	
3.	
4.	
5.	

Step 4: Superpower Fuel Gauge

At this point, you'll have at least 10 things marked with an X (more if you added extra powers). Congrats! Now write each of the X'd elements in the chart below. **These are fuel for your superpowers.**

Now, for each one, put an X in one of the three columns in the "Gut Monitor," measuring how you feel about the characteristic you've listed.

	Gut Monitor:	It's okay	Like it	Super-proud
	Example: I solve problems quickly.		X	
	Example: I'm extremely kind.			X
1.				
2.				
3.				
4.				
5.				
6.				
7.				
8.				
9.				
10.				

Step 5: Superpower Test Flight

It's mash-up time. Write five versions of your superpowers, putting the things you're most proud of above in your mental blender and seeing what comes out. Remember: there's no right or wrong here; it's just a test flight. After you have five, go back and mark them on the Gut Monitor.

	Gut Monitor:	It's okay	Like it	Super-proud
	Example: I use my sensitivity, kindness, and willingness to laugh to solve tough problems in new and fresh ways.		X	
1.				
2.				
3.				
4.				
5.				

Step 6: Here Are My Superpowers!

Now, what's most super about you? What's powerful? What makes you proud? **Write it down here.**

Congrats! You're well on your way to discovering your superpowers, and getting the clarity, confidence, and control you need to take those superpowers to work!

Tell us about what you found. Share your superpowers on our Facebook page at *www.Facebook.com/RedCapeRevolution*, or go to *www.RedCapeRevolution.com* and use the Contact page to email us directly.

What to Say to Build Confidence

Everything we say helps build—or destroy—others' confidence in us. Here's a list of words and phrases you can try in various situations to help you build better relationships and help others feel more confident in you. Try them out, and don't be surprised if along the way, you start feeling more confident in yourself, too.

What to Say to Connect Better

- "I'd like to make sure we're connecting well and that you have confidence in me and our work together. What do I need to do to achieve that goal?"

- "My observation is that you and [*name of someone else*] have a very strong working relationship. I'd like to have that kind of relationship with you someday. What helped the two of you learn to work so well together? What can I do to earn that relationship with you?"

- "I realized we don't know much about each other, and I'd like to change that. Could we meet for lunch sometime to get to know each other better?"

- "I am always interested in learning more about how people work and make decisions. Could we find 30 minutes to have a cup of coffee soon?"

- "I'm working on my goals and I'd appreciate your insights. Can we spend 20 minutes when I can share some thoughts with you and get your feedback?"

- [*To someone familiar with the person you're trying to get to know*] "I'd really like to develop a better relationship with [*name*]. What do you know about him/her that might help me?"

What to Say If You Think Others Aren't Confident in You

- "I'd observe you're not feeling as comfortable with me as I'd hoped. Is that an accurate perception? [*If they agree*] "I appreciate your honesty. I'd like to build your confidence in me. What can I do to help that?"

- "I don't know about you, but our [relationship/work together] isn't as smooth as I think we'd both like it to be. What can I do to fix that?"

- "It's important for me to build great relationships. On a scale of 1-10, with 10 being perfect, how would you rate ours? What do we need to do to get it to a 10?"

- *[If you're made an error]* "Looking back, I made a mistake when I did/said [*your situation/comments*]. I value our relationship. What can I do to get us on the right track again?"

What to Say When You Don't Have the Answers

- "I'll be honest with you—I'm unsure of how to respond here. I'd like to think on it a little. Can we talk again about it tomorrow morning?"

- "I don't know your [*situation/company*] well enough to answer that yet. Tell me more about [*ask for more details*]..."

- "What a good question! I don't have as equally good an answer, but I'd like to. Let me put some thought in it and let's talk again later."

- "Hmm. You've stumped me. Let's talk a minute about how we might figure this out."

What to Say to Demonstrate You Were Listening (And to Make People Feel Heard)

- "What I heard you say is..."

- "Let me play your comments back to you. You said..."

- "Did I understand you correctly when you explained that..."

- "Building on your idea, I'd suggest..."

- "So it seems like there are really three different issues going on here, which if I'm hearing you right, are..."

- "Is there anything we haven't talked about that you think I should know?"

What to Say to Demonstrate Your Credibility

- "In my experience, I've found..."

- "One of my colleagues recently shared a story with me where..."

- "In my observation..." [*What you observe through your experiences is always valid to share.*]

- "What I'm finding in the marketplace is..."

- "I hear what you're saying, and the other things to consider are..." [*Use "and" instead of "but"—"and" is inclusive, while "but" signals disagreement.*]

What to Say to Show Respect to Others and Still Respect Yourself

- "I'm honored to partner with you on this initiative."

- "I'm proud of what we've accomplished together."

- "It's great to see that our efforts together are paying off."

- "I value our partnership and I'm glad you and I [*or your company and my company*] have been successful together."

- "I'm so glad we've been able to bring our superpowers to work together!"

Questions to Create Conversations

As a professional coach, part of my craft involves the art and science of asking bigger, powerful questions—and then shutting up and listening to the answers. (The shutting up was the harder of the skills to learn.)

After you read this book, you may want to ask some bigger questions, too, of friends, colleagues, and even yourself. Questions can open up new, fresh conversations that lead to better solutions and greater understanding of how we all look at our work. Plus, pulling together a group to talk about things other than the weather, sports, or the latest scandal can be fun and energizing.

Also, if you're a manager or leader, using bigger questions like this can generate information that will help you understand your people better, break old patterns of communication and build better relationships in an instant. Add a powerful question to the start of a meeting, or use it to kick off a one-on-one session to shake things up. (Your people don't have to have read this book for most of these questions to work; however, it can be a good conversation starter. If you're interested in purchasing copies of this book for your team, contact us at *info@redcaperevolution.com* and ask for current bulk rates.)

Here are a few questions to create conversations:

- What's your reaction to the idea of a "Red Cape Revolution" at work? What needs to be revolutionized at our/your organization?

- What would you say are your superpowers? If you're not sure, how can you get clearer?

- You work with [colleague's name] quite a bit. In your observation, what would you say are [her/his] superpowers? Would you say [she/he] knows that?

- What's the biggest problem you see in our/your organization that your own superpowers could help solve?

- If you weren't worried about what anyone else would think, how would you start bringing your superpowers to work right now?

- What might change for you personally if you start bringing your superpowers to work more often?

- If you had a magic wand, what one thing would you change right now about your daily experience at work?

- What's the one thing that has made you the most proud in the past year at work?

- In what kind of situations are you most confident? How can you create more of those?

- If there were no consequences, how would you take more control of your career right now?

- What support do you need so you can bring your superpowers to work and make a bigger difference in your work and life?

A Message for Managers and Leaders: Ten Things Your People Want

It's my privilege to work with and speak to many ambitious, hard-working and energetic corporate professionals. They're often the up-and-coming talent, the get-it-done gang, and the backbone of a company's next generation of success. This book was written for, and with, them, and hopefully, these pages contain ideas for actions they can take themselves, with or without your support.

But they actually **want** your support—but in ways that might surprise you. As you think about discovering your own superpowers as a manager or leader, I also wanted you to be armed with the ten things top talent in many of today's successful organizations are collectively wishing for from you. Let's listen in to their words.

1. Trust me.

I know trust is especially hard these days—we're moving so fast that our default position is to assume we can't trust anything. But trust has now become the biggest gap in our relationship. I need you to take a leap and trust I'm competent, confident, and that I care. (If you don't think so, then trust me enough to tell me.) Also, did you know that according to recent research, trust generates oxytocin, the "feel good hormone," in both the person trusted and the person trusting. I could use some of that—how about you?

2. Ask me.

Stop assuming you know what I want in my career. When you're doing "strategic planning" or "talent review," please remember that I may have good ideas about how I can contribute to the organization's growth. Unless we're responding to a crisis, don't invest a lot of time in new processes or roles that impact me without asking me my ideas first. And feel free to challenge me with the big, hard questions—I can handle it. In the end, I'll probably do what you decide, but you'll get more energy from me and avoid stupid mistakes if you ask first.

3. Give me room.

For me, the carrot and the stick have lost their ability to influence me to do what you want, so stop trying to bribe me or scare me into action. Just tell me what you want to accomplish, but give me room to do the job the way I know I can. (Of course, to do this, go back to #1.)

4. Include me.

I know you know I'm busy, and I'll give you benefit of the doubt that you're not inviting me to sit in on some of your meetings and calls because you don't want me to waste my time. But how 'bout letting me decide? I love to feel included, to know you want me involved. Even if you include me with boundaries (like telling me in advance I have a voice, not a vote), I'll appreciate the invitation—even if I decline.

5. Connect me.

I can't be the only one wrestling with the same business challenges. Who else can I learn from? Who should I know to grow my career? Who inside our organization do I need to meet? Outside?? Your introductions and connections are like gold, and down deep, I long for community. Help me create it.

6. Leave me alone.

When I'm not working, leave me alone. Create a micro-culture in our group where I can go "unplugged" and not feel guilty. I know, I know, I'll have to change some of my own habits to make that work, but it'd be a big help if you'd support me in words and actions.

7. Share your stories.

How did you get to where you are? What were the lessons you learned along the way? What's the biggest mistake you made? Why are you still at this company? I know we're all busy, but your success stories are interesting to me—and your failure stories even more so. Not sure if I want to hear them? See #2.

8. Value me.

Most of us aren't getting huge raises or bonuses anymore, yet the costs of most everything keep going up. I need better to understand how I'm financially valued here—how my pay compares to others, how decisions are made about increases, promotions, and what other ways there are to be financially rewarded in exchange for the contributions I make here. Pay isn't everything to me, but I need the process to be mystery-free.

9. Re-recruit me.

Don't take me for granted. It's a myth that there are no jobs out there—the recruiters are finding me. I'm also thinking hard about my next step—and it might be to our competitor, my own company, or to a nonprofit, or someplace where I feel I will be making a bigger difference. If I can make more of a difference here, tell me so. Tell me why you want me here. Find out what's important to me, and help me see the intersection between my needs and the organization's.

10. Invest in me.

I hear you saying I'm your greatest asset, but from where I sit, it seems like my training opportunities have been trimmed back, and the budgets for me to attend outside events seem limited. There's more emphasis on connecting virtual rather than face-to-face, and that keeps me from meeting more people I can learn in this organization. To keep me, you'll need to invest in relevant development opportunities for me. That might mean money, but it might simply be investing your time in figuring out what's the best thing we can do for the available budget and time. Just the fact of you asking what kind of professional development I might value will go a long way toward me feeling more engaged, confident, and connected.

Darcy's Story & Superpower Statement

What makes Darcy most proud is knowing that her clients, readers, and audience consistently grow to greater levels of clarity, confidence, and control—all leading to better business and personal results. **She wants the same for you.**

With over 20 years' experience in talent management, employee engagement, change management, and communication strategy, Darcy has seen firsthand what it takes to move today's busy professionals to take action. As a principal, business leader, and senior consultant at a top HR consulting firm, her blue-ribbon client list included The Coca-Cola Company, The Home Depot, Verizon, and Wells Fargo.

Even with extensive success "on paper," Darcy sparked a revolution of her own when she abandoned a comfortable, six-figure executive salary and leadership post for the seemingly risky path of becoming an entrepreneur.

But that path didn't create itself. Darcy built it, carefully and strategically, fueled by listening to the whispers that gnawed at her, as they do so many others: "What's next for my career?", "What else is out there?", "Am I making a difference?", and the biggie, "Is this all there is?"

Finding no answers within her organization—even with all its resources—Darcy began hunting the solutions on her own, seeking out the sparks of inspiration. While working a 70-hour week, she invested her time, money, and energy in informal and formal development, including doing the hard, mentally challenging work to get clear about what she really wanted, and what the world needed from her unique talents and gifts.

The spark turned into flame when Darcy uncovered a new possibility: the intersection of where her old experience and new desires combined. She created and pitched an idea to launch an internal coaching program focused on high-potential performers and high-impact teams in her own company—one she'd lead, of course. The plan worked, and Darcy married the workplace she knew with the bigger impact she longed to make going forward.

Taking the Leap

After proving (mostly to herself!) what she could do, she took the leap and left the security of her big, brand-name company to launch her own leadership and workplace coaching firm. There, she focused her talents on helping people get clear about their career paths, build confidence to keep them moving forward, and take control to create the work and career change they need. She never looked back.

Now, in addition to writing her blog at *www.RedCapeRevolution.com* and coaching and mentoring individuals and teams, Darcy is a popular speaker. She has been invited to share her expertise with companies such as The Coca-Cola Company, General Electric, State Farm, Deloitte Consulting, and Cracker Barrel, as well as groups such as the International Association of Business Communicators (IABC) and the Public Relations Society of America (PRSA), among others.

She earned the Associate Certified Coach (ACC) credential from the International Coach Federation (ICF) and served as the president of the Georgia Coach Association, one of ICF's largest U.S. chapters. She's been cited in a number of media, including the *Atlanta Journal-Constitution*, CNN.com, TheLadders.com, the *Modesto Bee*, Ask Dale TV, ABCnews.com, Careerbuilder.com, and more.

To find out more, including how you can work with Darcy or invite her to speak at your workplace or professional organization, visit *www.RedCapeRevolution.com.*

Darcy's Superpower Statement

I hope you take the time to work through our Superpower Statement Generator and discover what your own unique superpowers are. The clarity, confidence, and control you gain from knowing what they are will amaze you.

I've done a lot of work on this for myself in the past several years. It didn't always look like this. At one time, it was a lot more timid and compromising and less fun. Now, it makes me smile from ear to ear. So, for your reference, not your comparison to your own, here is my Superpower Statement:

As chief instigator of the Red Cape Revolution,
Darcy Eikenberg serves our Community every day
by practicing her unique superpowers.

Watch as she:

Unlocks your perception of how unique, talented,
and uber-amazing you really are,
no matter what your story or what you do...

Zeroes in, using super-charged vision, on the fresh connections,
hidden abilities, and ready-to-explode opportunities
that live within our organizations and our lives,
seeing possibilities where others see brick walls...

Activates a powerful force field of positive, real-life messages,
creating a protective screen against the negative
and false assumptions about our workplaces,
our colleagues, and our lives...

Outfits aspiring rebels and leaders
with revolution-generating gear
including clarity, confidence, and control—
and launches others into action to transform
their workplace and their world.

One way I know that these superpowers are really mine is that when I read the above lines, I get energized. I get excited. I get edge-of-my-seat anxious to finish writing this book so you can create your own Superpower Statement.

Of course, when you read it, you may feel differently. Once colleague kindly said it wore her out. That's okay. They're not her superpowers, they're mine.

Each Superpower Statement will look different. Most will be shorter than mine—at least to start. Some will be action-specific, while others will convey more of a feeling or an idea. That's okay, too. As you start discovering your superpowers, you'll know when you've captured the right ones for you.

References & Resources

Here are the books and resources I've referenced along the way in these pages. I hope you'll check them out and be as inspired as I have been. For direct links, visit *www.RedCapeRevolution.com/BookBonus*.

Books I've Mentioned

- Tom Rath: *Strengthsfinder 2.0*

- Marcus Buckingham and Donald O. Clifton: *Now, Discover Your Strengths*

- Daniel Pink: *Drive: The Surprising Truth About What Motivates Us*

- Cheryl Richardson: *Take Time for Your Life: A Personal Coach's 7-Step Program for Creating the Life You Want*

- Steven Pressfield: *The War of Art: Break Through the Blocks and Win Your Inner Creative Battles* and *Do the Work*

- Tony Schwartz, Jean Gomes, and Catherine McCarthy: *Be Excellent at Anything: The Four Keys to Transforming the Way We Work and Live*

- Peggy Klaus: *Brag: The Art of Tooting Your Own Horn Without Blowing It*

Other Books That Inspire

Not every book that's inspired me made its way into these pages by name. But they all have done their part to feed my brain and ideas.

- Seth Godin: *Linchpin: Are You Indispensible?*; *Poke the Box*; and *The Dip: A Little Book that Teaches You When to Quit (and When to Stick).* Plus, don't miss Seth's mind-expanding blog at *www.SethGodin.com.*

- Rosamund Stone Zander and Benjamin Zander: *The Art of Possibility: Transforming Professional and Personal Life*

- William Bridges: *Managing Transitions: Making the Most of Change*

- Jack Canfield and Mark Victor Hansen: *The Aladdin Factor*

- Daniel Pink: *A Whole New Mind: Why Right-Brainers Will Rule the Future*

- Thomas J. Leonard: *The Portable Coach: 28 Sure-Fire Strategies for Business and Personal Success*

- Richard Carlson: *Don't Sweat the Small Stuff—and It's All Small Stuff*

- Todd Henry: *The Accidental Creative: How to Be Brilliant at a Moment's Notice*

- William Powers: *Hamlet's BlackBerry: A Practical Philosophy for Building a Good Life in the Digital Age*

Other Resources

As you discover your superpowers and start bringing them to work, you may find that you especially need to tap into other resources and especially Build Your Support Team (see Part 3). Here are some places you can find people who bring different superpowers to the table.

- ***To find a coach:*** I can't work with everyone I'd like to, although if you'd like to find out more, visit *www.RedCapeRevolution.com/WorkWithDarcy*. But I do believe everyone can benefit from working with a professionally trained and credentialed coach. The International Coach Federation (*www.CoachFederation.org*) is the leading professional organization of personal, corporate, and business coaches, and I've been a member and leader in my local chapter for years. Check the website for free tools on how to choose the right coach for you.

- ***To find a professional organizer:*** The National Association of Professional Organizers (NAPO; *www.NAPO.net*) is a great place to start to find someone to help in your neck of the woods.

- ***To hire a virtual assistant or specialty support:*** There's a growing population of professionally trained virtual assistants, in your area and around the world. AssistU.com and OfficeAngels.us are two virtual assistant groups I've used. Also, you can hire targeted, one-time, or ongoing technical or specialty help at Odesk.com or Elance.com.

- ***To hire a financial planner:*** Since I want to work with people who care about me and my ability to use my superpowers—not just people who want to make money off me—I'm a huge fan of fee-only financial planners, rather than planners who get paid on commission. Start with the National Association of Personal Financial Advisors (NAPFA, *www.NAPFA.org*). For me, the team at Ritter Daniher Financial Advisors (*www.ritterdaniher.com*) takes good care of my interests.

- ***To find an image consultant:*** The Association of Image Consultants International (*www.AICI.org*) is a great way to start to find a personal or corporate image expert in your area. Plus, go visit my business girlfriend Sarah Hathorn at Illustra Consulting (*www.IllustraConsulting.com*), whose combination of coaching, branding, and presence consulting helps people move forward fast.

- ***To find almost anything else in your area:*** Even though it's a paid site, I'm a fan of Angie's List (*www.AngiesList.com*). For a small monthly fee, you can search all kinds of local service providers, see ratings and reviews from other members, and use Angie's staff to help resolve issues. Also, don't hesitate to ask your friends and colleagues for referrals on LinkedIn and Facebook. There's nothing like a personal connection.

WHO'S HELPING YOU KEEP YOUR RED CAPE FLYING?

Be sure to share your stories about asking for and finding the right support for you. Tell us on Facebook at *www.Facebook.com/ RedCapeRevolution*, or send our team an email at *info@redcaperevolution.com*.

Talk to Us

Have a question? Hold a different opinion than what you've read here? Find an error, or have a suggestion about improving this book in the next edition?

Don't keep your brilliance to yourself. Talk to us.

The comments and insights from people like you help us continue to learn, grow, and share new and fresh insights with even more people around the world. It's great to hear different opinions and ideas that this book stimulates. It's not a problem to us; it's a present.

Email us at *info@RedCapeRevolution.com,* or go to *www.RedCapeRevolution.com* and use our Contact page.
Plus, you can share ideas on Facebook at *www.Facebook.com/ RedCapeRevolution* or tweet us on Twitter @RedCapeRev.
(We try our best to respond to comments and inquiries as soon as possible, although sometimes we need to click less, too.)
We look forward to hearing from you!

About Red Cape Revolution

The people at Red Cape Revolution strive to help everyday professionals discover their superpowers, bring them to their work, and make a bigger difference in their corners of the world.

Our vision is that we're at the heart of a movement—a revolution—redefining and recreating the rules around how we work today. Our leadership and workplace coaching, consulting, speaking, teaching and publishing work—plus the career and success tools and ideas shared at our hub, RedCapeRevolution.com—all aim to generate more personal clarity, confidence and control in our lives at work, no matter what's happening in any one economy, industry, or company.

We believe that when more of us start to confidently wear our red capes and bring our superpowers to work, not only will we improve our lives, but we'll strengthen our companies, our communities, and our world, too.

We welcome and appreciate your ideas and feedback at www.RedCapeRevolution.com.

A Word of Thanks

You can't complete a project like this book without all the right support along the way. I haven't always been good at recognizing when I need support, but hopefully am good at acknowledging it when I have it. That said, this is just a partial list, so apologies in advance for whatever tragic oversights exist.

First, to all the clients who have invested their time, money, and energy in me as their leadership and workplace coach, I am honored and humbled to be part of the changes you have made in your professional and often in your personal lives, too. Your stories and successes are a key part of this book.

To those I've met while speaking, and to the community of people who subscribe to my updates at *www.RedCapeRevolution.com* and read my blog, you'll likely see some familiar stuff in here, but you said you liked it the first time, so…

To Laura West of the Center for Joyful Business (*www.JoyfulBusiness.com*), who pushed me to finally admit I was really a writer (how did I ignore that all those years?). Laura challenged me to use my slightly offbeat voice and creative energy as a business asset instead of pushing it all away as a distraction, and it has made all the difference.

To Renée Paley Bain, Cheli Brown, and Susan Zographos, who offered amazing insights on the drafts of this book. To Donna Kozik and all who shared ideas and encouragement through her programs at *www.WriteWithDonna.com.*

To John Mayer, for reasons just he and I and maybe a few savvy fans know.

To me, for giving myself the gift of a January week in Seaside, Florida, to begin the process of putting this material on paper. To Michael and Niki Murphy, for the loan of their Georgia mountain cabin to finish the last 10 percent.

To my professional coaches all along the way: Pat White, MCC, Tony Klingmeyer, MCC, the aforementioned Laura West, PCC, and my informal coaches, like Charles Lewis, wait-and-see.

To all the innovators who inspired me from afar: Tony Schwartz, Peggy Klaus, Dan Pink, Seth Godin. (Well, I did stalk Dan up close at a conference and got him to sign *Drive,* but chickened out of my peppy banter about how we went to Northwestern together. And I did get to meet Seth by volunteering to work at an event he spoke at in Atlanta, but I did a crappy job of talking about my still-developing idea for Red Cape Revolution. Another chance, Dan and Seth?)

And of course, to Mom, Dad, and Dana—the strength of our family is the greatest superpower of them all.

Always,
Darcy
Atlanta, Georgia
December 2011

Wait—You're Not Done!

Don't Forget to Grab Your Special Bonus Resources

www.RedCapeRevolution.com/BookBonus

Now that you have lots of ideas about how to discover your superpowers and bring them to your work right now, we want you remind you there are even more tools out there for you. Grab your free resources at *www.RedCapeRevolution.com/BookBonus* to help you wear your red cape and start soaring through your career and life.

Here's what you'll find:

- Darcy's companion video, *Getting Started with the Red Cape Revolution*, will walk you through the book and make sure you grab the highlights! It's a good, brief overview and also a good reminder later when you need a refresher.

- Our Frequently Asked Questions (FAQs), updated regularly with answers to questions from readers just like you.

- A special link where you can send your questions about the ideas in the book directly to Darcy and her Red Cape Revolution team. It's your chance to get personal answers and attention that may change your own experiences at work.

- Invitations to ongoing events, workshops, and classes where you can continue to build your clarity, confidence, and control at work.

Plus, the Red Cape Revolution team adds special surprises and bonuses all the time, exclusive to readers of this book, so check it out today.

Finally, to keep up with the latest from the Red Cape Revolution, make sure to sign up at *www.RedCapeRevolution.com*, and start getting our Community News, with ideas and inspiration you can use in your worklife right now.

The world is waiting—start soaring today!